Asia Bible Commentary

MICAH

GLOBAL LIBRARY

Asia Bible Commentary Series

MICAH

Johan Ferreira

with Contextualization Consultant
Ruth House

General Editor
Federico G. Villanueva

Old Testament Consulting Editors
Yohanna Katanacho, Tim Meadowcroft, Joseph Shao

New Testament Consulting Editors
Steve Chang, Andrew Spurgeon, Brian Wintle

© 2017 by Johan Ferreira

Published 2017 by Langham Global Library
an imprint of Langham Creative Projects

Langham Partnership
PO Box 296, Carlisle, Cumbria CA3 9WZ, UK
www.langham.org

Published in partnership with Asia Theological Association

ATA
QCC PO Box 1454 – 1154, Manila, Philippines
www.ataasia.com

ISBNs:
978-1-78368-325-3 Print
978-1-78368-327-7 Mobi
978-1-78368-326-0 ePub
978-1-78368-328-4 PDF

Johan Ferreira has asserted his right under the Copyright, Designs and Patents Act, 1988 to be identified as the Author of this work.

All rights reserved. No part of this publication may be reproduced, stored in a retrieval system or transmitted, in any form or by any means, electronic, mechanical, photocopying, recording or otherwise, without the prior written permission of the publisher or the Copyright Licensing Agency.

Unless otherwise stated, Scripture quotations are from the New International Version, copyright © 2011. Used by permission. All rights reserved.

All images, unless otherwise stated, are © Johan Ferreira

British Library Cataloguing in Publication Data
A catalogue record for this book is available from the British Library

ISBN: 978-1-78368-325-3

Cover & Book Design: projectluz.com

Langham Partnership actively supports theological dialogue and an author's right to publish but does not necessarily endorse the views and opinions set forth, and works referenced within this publication or guarantee its technical and grammatical correctness. Langham Partnership does not accept any responsibility or liability to persons or property as a consequence of the reading, use or interpretation of its published content.

To all messengers of the Lord
in the rural areas of Asia
who faithfully bring the message of the Lord

CONTENTS

Commentary

Series Preface ix
Authors' Preface xi
List of Abbreviations xiii
Introduction 1
Micah 1–3: The Message of Destruction 17
Micah 4-5: The Message of Restoration 69
Micah 6–7: The Message of Reconciliation 107
Selected Bibliography 145

Topics

The Role of Israel with Respect to the Nations 23
Impending Judgment upon the Church 31
Injustices within the Church Today 37
Worldly Values among Christians 42
The Remnant 47
Worldliness among Christian Leaders 53
Deceitful Preachers 56
False and True Prophets 64
A Bright Future for Asia 79
Christianity and Peace 89
Bethlehem as the Birthplace of Jesus 97
Christian Revival and Church Renewal 103
Genuine Repentance Is Required 118
Micah and Preaching 124
Micah as a Model for Today 138

SERIES PREFACE

In recent years, we have witnessed one of the greatest shifts in the history of world Christianity. It used to be that the majority of Christians lived in the West. But now the face of world Christianity has changed beyond recognition. Christians are now evenly distributed around the globe. This has implications for the interpretation of the Bible. In our case, we are faced with the task of interpreting the Bible from within our respective contexts. This is in line with the growing realization that every theology is contextual. Our understanding of the Bible is influenced by our historical and social locations. Thus, even the questions that we bring into our reading of the Bible will be shaped by our present realities. There is a need therefore to interpret the Bible for our own contexts.

The Asia Bible Commentary (ABC) series addresses this need. In line with the mission of the Asia Theological Association Publications, we have gathered Asian evangelical Bible scholars in Asia to write commentaries on each book of the Bible. The mission is to "produce resources that are biblical, pastoral, contextual, missional, and prophetic for pastors, Christian leaders, cross-cultural workers, and students in Asia." Although the Bible can be studied for different reasons, we believe that it is given primarily for the edification of the body of Christ (2 Tim 3:16–17). The ABC series is designed to help pastors in their sermon preparation, cell group leaders or lay leaders in their Bible study groups, Christian students in their study of the Bible, and Christians in general in their efforts to apply the Bible in their respective contexts.

Each commentary begins with an introduction that provides general information about the book's author and original context, summarizes the main message or theme of the book, and outlines its potential relevance to a particular Asian context. The introduction is followed by an exposition that combines exegesis and application. Here, we seek to speak to and empower Christians in Asia by using our own stories, parables, poems, and other cultural resources as we expound the Bible.

The Bible is actually Asian in that it comes from ancient West Asia and there are many similarities between the world of the Bible and traditional Asian cultures. But there are also differences that we need to explore in some depth. That is why the commentaries also include articles or topics in which we bring specific issues in Asian church, social, and religious contexts into dialogue with relevant issues in the Bible. We do not seek to resolve every tension but rather

Micah

to allow the text to illumine the context and vice versa, acknowledging that in the end we do not have all the answers to every mystery.

May the Holy Spirit who inspired the writers of the Bible bring light to the hearts and minds of all who use these materials, to the glory of God and to the building up of the churches!

Federico G. Villanueva

General Editor

AUTHORS' PREFACE

It has been both a privilege and a challenge to study, to teach, and to write a commentary on the book of Micah. God's word is always invigorating, "reviving the soul, rejoicing the heart, and enlightening the eyes." But also, at the same time, it exposes our deep-seated sins and various short-comings, reminding us that we all "fall short of the glory of God." Therefore, Micah is all the more precious since it reveals a God who delights in showing mercy and who throws our sins into the depths of the sea.

The book of Micah is like a window into the literature, the world, and the message of the Old Testament prophets. Since the book is relatively short, it may be studied in-depth from the pulpit, in the classroom, at Bible Study, or at a special seminar. Congregations and students will gain a thorough understanding not only of Micah, but also of Old Testament theology and especially the prophetic books in general.

More importantly, the book of Micah contains an urgent message for the church in Asia today. In many ways, the current state of the church reflects the situation of Israel during the time of Micah. Idolatry, syncretism, worldliness, and ignorance of God's ways are widespread throughout Asian Christianity. It will not escape God's judgment. However, we are confident that God will once again revive his church. The book of Micah gives us hope that Asian Christians, especially preachers and teachers, will rediscover the gospel and through the power of the Spirit will once again become courageous messengers of the Lord Jesus Christ. There is a desperate need for the church and for Christians to study the book of Micah and take its message to heart.

The commentary is based on a careful reading of the Hebrew text. In line with the practical orientation of the commentary, we have not engaged in much technical discussion of academic issues and have adopted a user-friendly (non-scientific) transliteration of the Hebrew words when necessary. All illustrations and photos are supplied by the authors, unless otherwise acknowledged. We would like to thank the Asia Theological Association for giving us this opportunity to contribute to the Asia Bible Commentary Series. We also express our gratitude to our students who have joined us in the study of the text of Micah.

Johan Ferreira and Ruth House

LIST OF ABBREVIATIONS

BOOKS OF THE BIBLE

Old Testament
Gen, Exod, Lev, Num, Deut, Josh, Judg, Ruth, 1–2 Sam, 1–2 Kgs, 1–2 Chr, Ezra, Neh, Esth, Job, Ps/Pss, Prov, Eccl, Song, Isa, Jer, Lam, Ezek, Dan, Hos, Joel, Amos, Obad, Jonah, Mic, Nah, Hab, Zeph, Hag, Zech, Mal

New Testament
Matt, Mark, Luke, John, Acts, Rom, 1–2 Cor, Gal, Eph, Phil, Col, 1–2 Thess, 1–2 Tim, Titus, Phlm, Heb, Jas, 1–2 Pet, 1–2–3 John, Jude, Rev

BIBLE TEXTS AND VERSIONS

Divisions of the canon
NT	New Testament
OT	Old Testament

Ancient texts and versions
LXX	Septuagint
MT	Masoretic Text

Modern versions
ESV	English Standard Version
KJV	King James Version
NASB	New American Standard Bible
NET	New English Translation
NIV	New International Version
NLT	New Living Translation
NRSV	New Revised Standard Version

Journals, Reference Works, and Series
AB	Anchor Bible
ABC	Asia Bible Commentary
CBQ	*Catholic Biblical Quarterly*
JBL	*Journal of Biblical Literature*
JSOTSup	*Journal for the Study of Old Testament Supplement Series*

Micah

NICOT	New International Commentary on the Old Testament
TOTC	Tyndale Old Testament Commentaries
WBC	Word Biblical Commentary

INTRODUCTION

The beginning of the twenty-first century is a time of change – and even of crisis – in the world and especially in Asia. We are witnessing a rapid and dramatic shift in the balance of economic and political power from the West to the East, as well as the rise of several global and regional crises such as inequality, pollution, terrorism, and climate change. This uncertain state of affairs inevitably increases anxiety and raises many questions about the future. In particular, can the church discover a prophetic voice to address contemporary issues and provide confidence for the present and hope for the future? A careful study of the book of Micah will reveal that there is indeed a word from God for the church in Asia today.

The book of Micah was composed during a time of crisis and change in the history of Israel and Judah. In 722 BC the capital of Israel, Samaria, fell into the hands of the Assyrians, which meant exile for the northern ten tribes and the demise of the kingdom of Israel. Then, around 130 years later in 586 BC, the capital of Judah, Jerusalem, was destroyed by the Babylonians, resulting in exile for the southern two tribes and the end of the Davidic dynasty. The Sargon II cuneiform inscription[1] of the sacking of Samaria and the burnt house with Babylonian arrow heads unearthed on the Ophel in Jerusalem provide graphic reminders of these devastating events in the history of the Old Testament people of God. After the great success engendered by the reigns of David and Solomon, why did the Israelite kingdom and the Davidic house disintegrate into a mound of ruins? Was there still hope for the great project of global blessing envisioned by the Abrahamic Covenant? Could ruins be rebuilt and could lost tribes be re-gathered?

METHODOLOGY

Over the last 100 years critical scholars have expressed a range of views about the context, compositional history, and message of the book of Micah, views which have often been contradictory and mutually exclusive. In general, many scholars have regarded chapters 1 to 3 as dating back to the time of Micah in

---

1. The text is extant on several cuneiform prisms housed in the British Museum (item WA 22505, not on display) in the Louvre, in the Iraq Museum in Baghdad, and in the Israel Museum in Jerusalem. For a translation of the inscription, see James B. Pritchard, *The Ancient Near East. Volume 1: An Anthology of Texts and Pictures* (Princeton, NJ: Princeton University Press, 1973), 195–198.

the eighth century BC, whereas the rest of the book stems from the post-exilic period. Consequently, the message of the book, so it is argued by some, is often inconsistent oscillating between oracles of judgment and salvation. However, these views are problematic, since there is simply not enough evidence to support the elaborate reconstructions of hypothetical sources or layers of tradition, let alone dating those sources to specific periods of time. Of course, presuppositions often determine the results of one's analysis and interpretation. The approach of this commentary is determined by its purpose, which is to supply resource material for pastors, teachers, counselors, and theological students. In line with the aims of the Asia Bible Commentary series, this study employs a canonical approach in its analysis of the book of Micah.

In the past, most scholars have used the historical-critical method in the exegetical study of the Old Testament text. Evangelicals have used a less "critical" methodology and have preferred the term "grammatical-historical" method (the latter term is especially used in Reformed circles). Indeed, the historical-critical method has been an important and valuable tool in biblical interpretation. Nevertheless, this method has a basic weakness in that it cannot deal adequately with questions of context and theology. In the last two decades, there has been a move away from history to focus on the narrative or the text. However, as historical criticism has been inadequate by ignoring the narrative framework of the text, a purely narrative approach is also inadequate as it divorces the text from its historical context. A canonical approach, on the other hand, incorporates the best aspects of both historical criticism and narrative criticism and yet is internally consistent as a scientific method of reading.[2] The canonical approach emphasizes the importance of reading a text in the context of whole narratives, thus, taking on board the insights of narrative criticism. But in addition to a purely narrative approach it emphasizes the unity of the Bible or the interdependence of texts (intertextuality). On the other hand, the canonical approach also takes history seriously by highlighting or trying to identify the concerns of the community for which the text was written. The interpreter is primarily concerned with theological questions and sees himself

---

2. See Brevard Childs, *Introduction to the Old Testament as Scripture* (Philadelphia: Fortress, 1979), and *Biblical Theology of the Old and New Testaments: Theological Reflection on the Christian Bible* (Minneapolis: Fortress, 1992), and J. A. Sanders, *Canon and Community: A Guide to Canonical Criticism* (Philadelphia: Fortress, 1984), 45: "Canonical criticism honors and incorporates the tools as well as the sound results of literary criticism, archaeology, and philology, especially where they assist in fleshing out the historical and sociological contexts of ancient communities which shaped and were addressed by the biblical texts."

INTRODUCTION

or herself as standing within the same tradition as that of the Jewish and early Christian communities.

So perhaps most importantly, the canonical approach emphasizes the importance of purpose – the why, not just the how of reading. The question of methodology cannot be separated from one's own presuppositions in approaching the text. R. W. L. Moberly has stated the issue well, "Rather, the crucial question, which is prior to questions of method and sets the context for them, is that of purpose and goal. To put it simply, how we use the Bible depends on why we use the Bible."[3] In canonical criticism the "why" question, or the interpreter's pre-understanding, is stated clearly right at the beginning of the interpretive process. The text is read as authoritative revelation to provide illumination and guidance for the community in which the interpreter stands. Childs prefers to talk of canonical criticism not as a method *per se*, but rather as defining an attitude towards the Scripture. The interpreter reads the text as a Christian and does not merely act as a neutral observer of the text. Most distinctively, a canonical approach, as the term implies, places the emphasis on reading the text within the framework or context of the canon. As canon, the text gives direction for the reader in his or her search for meaning and authenticity. This wider framework provides the major context for interpreting a particular text and reflects the hermeneutical principle of the Reformation – *Scriptura Scripturae interpres* (Scripture is its own interpreter).

Therefore, the text stands at the center of the hermeneutical approach, not the history behind the text or the reader in front of the text. But still, the text is interpreted in the context of the historical situation as outlined by the text – history is important since the word of God addresses people in their historical and existential situations. Furthermore, the text is interpreted as a whole and within its canonical context – it is only in this framework that we have received the text and that we have access to the text. And, finally, the text is interpreted within the context of, and for the benefit of, a believing community, which is taking the purpose of reading seriously (theology) – the interpreting process is not an isolated academic exercise (see Figure 1).

---

3. R. W. L. Moberly, *The Old Testament of the Old Testament: Patriarchal Narratives and Mosaic Yahwism* (Minneapolis: Fortress, 1992), 2.

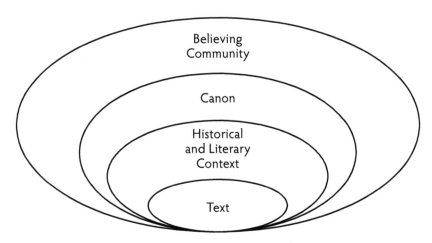

Figure 1. The Canonical Approach to Reading Scripture

DATING AND HISTORICAL CONTEXT

When it comes to the dating of the book of Micah, two time periods must be distinguished in order to clarify the book's historical setting (see Figure 3). The first period relates to the life and prophetic ministry of the historical prophet, Micah. The second period concerns the date of the composition or final editing of the book of Micah. According to the editorial notation appended at the beginning of the book, the prophet Micah prophesied during the reigns of the Judean kings Jotham (r. 750–732), Ahaz (r. 735–715), and Hezekiah (r. 715–686). This time frame dates the ministry of the prophet to the latter half of the eighth century (c. 750–700 BC). There is no reason to doubt the accuracy of the notation; the imagery, geographical references, and rhetorical situation in the book are consistent with such a time frame. The canonical compilers did not hesitate to locate the prophecy against this late eighth century background. However, perhaps equally important for interpreting the book, is the setting of the composition or final editing of the prophet's speeches as a whole in literary form, which is later than the ministry of the historical prophet. In this regard, we may make two observations which will serve as the basis of our presupposition regarding the dating of the final editing of the book. Firstly, the title gives the earliest possible date for the composition of the book, which is after the reign of Hezekiah and thus implies a date later than 686 BC. Secondly, the latest possible date for the appearance of the book may be determined by the reference to the book of Micah in Jeremiah 26:18 which implies a date before the year 610 BC.

Introduction

The introductory formula in Jeremiah, "This is what the Lord Almighty says," introducing the quote from Micah 3:12 demonstrates that the speeches of the prophet Micah have already been codified and accepted as Scripture by the time of Jeremiah's trial at around 610 BC. Therefore, the most plausible suggestion is that the book of Micah was edited into its current shape during the reign of Manasseh (c. 687–642), Hezekiah's successor.

The most significant implication of this general time frame is that the book of Micah was composed after the fall of Samaria in 722 BC, but before the fall of Jerusalem in 586 BC. In interpreting and preaching from the book of Micah this time frame regarding the events of the Assyrian and Babylonian exile needs to be carefully considered. Based on the available evidence, it is hard to be any more specific than this; nevertheless, this time frame provided by the canonical context is sufficient for a confident and meaningful interpretation of the book.

The general conditions of Israel and especially of Judah during this time are described in 2 Kings 15–20 and 2 Chronicles 27–32. When we read the accounts, we note that all the kings of Israel "did evil in the eyes of the Lord" (2 Kgs 15:9, 18, 24, 28; 17:2). The sin of Jeroboam, who set up two golden calves in Dan and Bethel to consolidate his kingdom, is particularly singled out. According to the account of 2 Kings, pagan shrines and foreign worship were prevalent across the land. Archaeological discoveries of idolatrous figurines dating to the eighth century and the Samaria Ostraca inscribed with many Israelite names containing the compound of the Canaanite deity "Ba'al" demonstrate the accuracy of the reports in 2 Kings. In addition to prevalent idolatrous practices, the other problem that frequently appears in the account of 2 Kings is the political treachery or the cruelty of the leaders of the northern kingdom. We often read of rebellion and murder among the nobility (see 2 Kgs 15:10, 14–16, 25, 30). Evidently, Israel failed miserably in terms of keeping God's covenant and establishing a righteous society. Therefore, because of their sins against the Lord according to the writer of 2 Kings, the northern kingdom fell into the hands of Assyria and was carried away into captivity. This disaster happened in 722 BC when Samaria, which was a strongly fortified city, succumbed after a three-year siege by the Assyrian king Shalmaneser V. The Assyrian clay prism, now held in the British Museum, provides another account of the fall of Samaria. It attributes the victory over Samaria to Shalmaneser's successor, Sargon II, who boasts in cuneiform writing, "I besieged and captured Samaria, and carried off 27,290 of its inhabitants as booty" (compare 2 Kgs 17:5–6).[4]

---

4. Pritchard, *The Ancient Near East. Volume 1: An Anthology of Texts and Pictures*, 195.

The kings of Judah during the time of Micah were a little better than the kings of Israel. According to the biblical account, Jotham, even though he did not remove all idolatry from the southern kingdom, "did what was right in the eyes of the Lord" (2 Kgs 15:34). His successor Ahaz, however, followed the ways of the kings of Israel and "did not do what was right in the eyes of the Lord" (2 Kgs 16:2–4). Hezekiah, who secured Judah's continuity after the demise of the northern kingdom, was a much better king. He not only "did what was right in the eyes of the Lord," but also removed idolatry from Judah (2 Kgs 18:3–5), cleansed the temple, and restored true worship (2 Chr 29). Hezekiah, through the support of the prophet Isaiah, also stared down the attack by Sennacherib upon Jerusalem (2 Chr 32) to gain an unexpected victory for Judah. His broad wall and water tunnel hewn through bedrock (2 Kgs 20:20; 2 Chr 32:2–5), constructed to fortify Jerusalem against the Assyrian threat, can still be seen in Jerusalem today (see Figure 8). With Manasseh, however, Judean society became idolatrous and harsh (2 Kgs 21:1–18; 2 Chr 33:1–20). According to the writer of 2 Chronicles, at this time Judah "did more evil than the nations the Lord had destroyed before the Israelites" (2 Chr 33:9). Therefore, to conclude, we may note three things about the historical context of Micah: there were widespread idolatry, a prosperous economy, and a chaotic political situation in the northern kingdom.

CANONICAL CONTEXT

As mentioned above, our interpretation of the book of Micah is set within the context of the canon. Therefore, interpreting a passage involves a process of reading it in the context of an ever-expanding narrative framework until it is understood in accordance with the overall message or plot of the Bible. Firstly, a passage is interpreted in light of the overall message of the subsection within the book, and then within the overall message of the book as a whole. Secondly, the passage is then interpreted within the context of the canonical section where it is found within the Bible, viz. the Book of the Twelve (or the Minor Prophets). And then, thirdly, the passage is finally interpreted in terms of its overall context within the Old Testament and New Testament Scriptures of the Christian canon. There is no doubt that the eighth century prophet Micah saw himself as standing within the traditions of the Abrahamic and Mosaic covenants and articulated a message that was consistent with those traditions. Likewise, the editors of the book of Micah and the Hebrew Bible redacted the text to be consistent with the form and message of the other eleven prophets

Introduction

in the Book of the Twelve and intentionally placed it in its canonical location after Jonah and before Nahum as an eighth century prophet.[5] Therefore, in the canonical approach the interpretation of a passage cannot be restricted to the historical circumstances of eighth century Israel. Furthermore, as Christians, following the example of the New Testament writers, we interpret the book of Micah in light of the life, death, and resurrection of Jesus, who came to fulfill Old Testament prophecy and establish God's rule in the world.

The first concentric circle of reading, therefore, places the book of Micah within the context of the Minor Prophets or the Book of the Twelve. More recently scholars have recognized that this last section of the Prophets in the Hebrew Bible was edited together with many literary links and shared theological themes. There even appears to be design in the order in which the collection was arranged. It covers the major period of prophetic activity in Israel's history from the ninth to the fifth century BC and provides a summary of the canonical prophetic tradition. Although the twelve books address different circumstances and periods, and reflect the diverse characters of the individual prophets, the Book of the Twelve can be studied as a coherent collection. Many scholars have pointed out that it was most probably published as one scroll roughly equivalent in length to that of the Major Prophets. Therefore, although individual books contain their own unique theme and message, they all form part of the bigger work and contribute to the message of the prophets as a whole.

We may use the key text in Haggai 1:13 as a window into the main themes of the Book of the Twelve, "Then Haggai, the LORD's messenger, gave this message of the LORD to the people: 'I am with you,' declares the LORD." In short, the collection is about the *message* of the Lord and the *messenger* of the Lord. The main message, that the true messengers bring, is that God, despite Israel's sin and weakness, will be with his people. Of course, this promise has been fulfilled with the coming of the Lord Jesus Christ, who is Immanuel ("God with us"). As such, the Book of the Twelve, including Micah, is interesting to preachers and teachers of God's word. It deals with the kind of circumstances and challenges that preachers of all ages face as they minister the Word and serve the church. It also describes the kind of preacher that God is raising up for his church and world. We may propose the following three-fold division or general structure for the Book of the Twelve.

---

5. On reading the *Book of the Twelve* within its canonical context, see Paul R. House, *The Unity of the Twelve* (Sheffield: Sheffield Academic Press, 1990).

Overall Theme:		
Because Israel sinned, God punishes Israel with destruction and exile; yet through this apparent failure, God will bring restoration to his people as well as blessing to all the nations fulfilling the intention of the Abrahamic covenant.		
Section One: Israel's sin through violation of the divine covenant	Section Two: Israel's salvation through divine punishment	Section Three: Israel's service through divine restoration
1) Hosea	5) Jonah	9) Zephaniah
2) Joel	6) Micah	10) Haggai
3) Amos	7) Nahum	11) Zechariah
4) Obadiah	8) Habakkuk	12) Malachi

This outline articulates the three main aspects or themes of the collection of prophecies. Firstly, Israel sinned and violated the covenant. The first four books in the series highlight Israel's sin in violating the stipulations of the covenant. Therefore, secondly, God will punish Israel for her unfaithfulness. The next four books emphasize God's salvation, which paradoxically will follow punishment. But, thirdly, and most importantly, because God is faithful in love and grace, he will restore his people who in turn will bring blessing to all the nations. The final four books, in which the restoration of the temple becomes a dominant theme, focus on the responsibilities and the new role of God's covenant people. It is interesting to note that this general three-part outline is also seen in Paul's epistle to the Romans, which sequentially deals with the issues of sin, salvation, and service.

As can be seen from the outline above, the book of Micah lies in the middle section of the Book of the Twelve. This section deals with divine salvation, which ironically will happen as a consequence of divine punishment, seen very clearly in the preceding story of the prophet Jonah. Although the theme of punishment is a dominant one in the book of Micah, within God's overall plan of salvation it will facilitate Israel's restoration. God's ways of working are indeed very different from those of humans. Hence, the book concludes with the exclamation, "Who is a God like you?", which is also the meaning of the Hebrew name "Micah." In the New Testament, this question is most fully answered in the person and work of the Lord Jesus Christ.

Introduction

PROPHETS AND PROPHECY

It is essential for interpreting the book of Micah that the modern reader understands the role of Old Testament prophets and the nature of prophecy. The message of Old Testament prophecy is multifaceted and is much more than simply a prediction of future events. Interpreters have discerned two aspects in the message of the prophets, viz. forth-telling and fore-telling. Of first importance, the prophets articulated God's view or assessment of their surrounding society. There is a divine critique of contemporary society, which often involved a recollection of God's past action in history for his people and the demands of the covenant. The prophets were proclaimers – or forth-tellers – of the covenant and called God's people to repentance and faith, much like preachers today. As such, the prophets acted as witnesses for God. When one analyzes the content of biblical prophecy it appears that the bulk of the prophets' message can be characterized as "forth-telling." It is also this aspect of speaking on God's behalf that is to the fore in the definition of the role of the prophet in the Bible (see Exod 4:14–16; 7:1–2; Deut 18:15–22; Jer 1:4–10). The prophet simply speaks what God wants him or her to say. But, secondly, there was also proclamation of future things or the "fore-telling" of things to come in the message of the prophets. The prophets not only reminded God's people of the past, they also announced new things that were going to happen in the future. They were much more than proclaimers of the covenant; they also predicted "new things" (see Isa 43:18–19; 48:6; 65:17; Jer 31:31–33; Ezek 36:26). Even though fore-telling is less pronounced than forth-telling in prophetic literature, the emphasis being much more on present obligation (*paraenesis*), fore-telling nevertheless encapsulates an integral element of biblical prophecy. Future woe or weal, judgment or salvation, will come about through the direct intervention of God in history. The fulfillment of predictive prophecy demonstrates that the events in question are extremely important in terms of salvation history and did not simply happen by chance or through mere human instrumentality. The divine or miraculous element in prophecy (fore-telling) is an essential element of biblical revelation.

Thus, we may note that predictive prophecy (fore-telling) has three main purposes. Firstly, predictions of coming judgment serve as warnings to the listeners. If people do not repent, disaster is certain. Secondly, predictions of future blessing serve to encourage faith and trust. Since God is going to protect his people and bring about salvation for them, they should not lose heart but should persevere in their commitment. And, thirdly, the fulfillment of predictive prophecy indicates that the event has come about as the result of

God's activity in history. The event did not happen by chance, but is related to salvation history (see Isa 43:11–13; 45:20–21; 46:9–11; 48:3–8).

However, in order to avoid misunderstanding, it is important for modern interpreters to realize that the message of the prophets or the prophetic genre incorporates much more than prediction. In this way, there is not much difference between the message of the biblical prophets and the contemporary preacher. The biblical prophet articulated God's word – whether it was forth-telling or fore-telling.[6] So too, the task of the modern preacher is to proclaim God's word, which may relate to the past (i.e. what God has done in history, for example the life, death, and resurrection of Jesus), to the present (i.e. what God requires now, for example, people must repent and believe the gospel), or to the future (i.e. what God is going to do, for example, Jesus is coming back). The first two aspects incorporate forth-telling, whereas the last aspect incorporates fore-telling. Of course, the main difference between the Old Testament prophets and the contemporary preacher is that the writings (Canonical Scripture) of the biblical prophets are divinely inspired, and hence, are the authoritative and infallible word of God. Contemporary preaching must conform to and be tested against this standard.

Also, in interpreting biblical prophecy about future events the reader should be aware that it is often conditional on the response of people. For example, scholars often use the Deuteronomistic[7] prophecies regarding the exile to illustrate this point. According to the language of Deuteronomy 28:15–68, the exile is not an inevitable event; Israel's obedience may prevent the coming of this disaster. The exile is conditional upon disobedience, hence the *apodosis* (the "then" clause) is predicated on a *protasis* (the "if" clause), "if (*'im*) you do not obey" (see 2 Kgs 17:13–14; 2 Chr 36:15–21). Another clear example of the conditional nature of prophecy is seen in Jonah's preaching to the city of Nineveh, "Forty more days and Nineveh will be overthrown" (Jonah 3:4). However, the repentance of the people of Nineveh averted the judgment and the prophecy was not fulfilled. In fact, the conditional nature of many prophecies about judgment is an intrinsic element of biblical prophecy, since its aim is to encourage people to repent and respond appropriately to God's word. If judgment is unavoidable, then there is no point to warn people to

---

6. The role of the "prophet" and the nature of "prophecy" in the New Testament are similar to the Old Testament understanding.
7. Scholars use the term "Deuteronomist" to refer to the editor(s) of the historical books Deuteronomy, Joshua, Judges, 1 and 2 Samuel, and 1 and 2 Kings. These books contain many similar themes and concerns.

change their ways. Prophecies about judgment serve as warnings and hence may be averted when people repent. Consequently, biblical prophecy is not fatalistic, but allows much room for human responsibility.

One should further note that biblical prophecy often has more than one fulfillment, which is referred to as the multiple fulfillment of prophecy. Another way of understanding this principle is that biblical prophecies are often fulfilled through a process of development rather than one decisive event. Again, we may cite the Deuteronomist prophecies about exile as an example. These prophecies were fulfilled with respect to the northern kingdom when it was carried into exile by the Assyrians in 722 BC, and then again with respect to the southern kingdom when it was carried into exile by the Babylonians in 586 BC. But more precisely, the exile of both the northern and southern kingdoms happened through a series of events; it was gradual rather than immediate. Samaria lost its outlying provinces before the city fell after a siege of three years, and Jerusalem experienced a series of exiles from 604 to 579 BC.

Finally, another important aspect of Old Testament prophecy that requires careful study and reflection whether forth-telling or fore-telling, is its poetic nature. Prophecy, by and large, is expressed in poetry, and as such, often does not articulate a detailed or literalistic description of past, present, or future events. Rather, prophecy comes through the media of poetic imagery, symbolism, and metaphor which are by nature open to a range of possible and legitimate interpretations. Therefore, the study of Old Testament prophecy is at the same time a study of Old Testament or Hebrew poetry.[8]

PREACHING FROM THE PROPHETS

The role of preachers in the church today is similar to the role of the Old Testament prophet, except that today's preachers do not receive or proclaim new revelation. Again, our commitment to the canon as the word of God determines our position. According to the Reformed and evangelical doctrine of Scripture the canon is closed. Apart from this important difference, the modern-day preacher like the Old Testament prophet proclaims and applies God's word within a specific context in order that people may live according to God's will. Contemporary preachers and teachers may, of course, receive

---

8. On the characteristics of Hebrew poetry, see David L. Petersen and Kent Harold Richards, *Interpreting Hebrew Poetry* (Minneapolis: Fortress, 1992). James L. Kugel, *The Idea of Biblical Poetry: Parallelism and Its History* (New Haven: Yale University Press, 1981). Also see, Federico Villanueva, *Psalms 1–72*, Asia Bible Commentary Series (Carlisle, UK: Langham, 2016), 7–10.

new insights or enlightenment through the Spirit on how God's word applies to their specific situation. The meaning of God's word, although multifaceted, does not change and must be interpreted according to its literary and historical context. However, the application of biblical truth varies according to our current needs and contexts, and must be conveyed in language that is understandable to the hearers. The necessity for contextualized application and communication highlights the urgent need for preachers and teachers who understand both God's word and the society in which they minister. Therefore, preachers and teachers must carefully study both God's word and their societal context in order to bring a message that is biblically accurate as well as contextually relevant. In addition, they must depend on the illumination and enablement of the Spirit as they carry out their urgent responsibility.

Walter C. Kaiser in his book, *Back to the Future: Hints for Interpreting Biblical Prophecy* (2003), has given us some very useful principles for interpreting prophecy. He lists the following:

1) Focus on the living God
2) Focus on the Lord Jesus Christ
3) Focus on the command/encouragement associated with the prophecy
4) Focus on the historical-biblical past

Furthermore, in light of our analysis above, we may add the following three principles:

5) Reflect on the poetic medium of prophecy (e.g. notice parallelism, the mood, the main point, and the imagery and metaphors used in the poem)
6) Reflect on the distinction between forth-telling and fore-telling in prophecy (e.g. which element is to the fore?)
7) Reflect on the fulfillment of predictive prophecy (e.g. consider multiple fulfillments, then and now)

Once the preacher understands the main concerns of the text, he or she must construct a message within the canonical framework of Scripture (i.e. salvation history) with relevant contextual application.

THEME, OUTLINE, AND PURPOSE

Understanding the major theme, basic outline, and intended purpose of a literary work is crucial for interpreting the details of the narrative. In general,

INTRODUCTION

ancient authors did not write arbitrarily, but were erudite writers who constructed their texts according to definite goals. This sophistication certainly applies to biblical literature. Therefore, from the perspective of the preacher, grasping the major theme of a book is crucial for clearly communicating its content. Since every passage or literary unit relates directly to the overall theme and purpose of the book, the preacher must constantly recall the book's theme and purpose. Details of the text must be interpreted in light of the book's overarching concerns. Furthermore, the application of the text to the current context must be consistent with the main purpose of the original author or editors. Therefore, understanding the theme, outline, and purpose of the text will give the preacher confidence, clarity, and a useful tool in communicating the prophetic message to hearers today.

We may suggest the following theme for the book of Micah. Although God is punishing Israel's sin, yet God, through his king, will forgive and revive his people, bringing peace to the whole world (Micah 7:18–20). In other words, although there are different kinds of prophetic material in the book covering a number of matters, there is a consistent theme that provides unity to the whole. The first section of the book highlights God's judgment upon Israel and Judah's idolatry, injustice, and covenant unfaithfulness (chapters 1 to 3). The second half of the book announces that God will still restore his people, through a promised deliverer from Bethlehem (chapters 4 to 5). This section contains the core message of the book, providing hope for a much better future. God's restoration does not only relate to Israel and Judah but to the world, encompassing salvation for all people. The final section reiterates previous themes and especially calls for repentance and faith on the part of the covenant people (chapters 6 to 7). As can be seen from this basic outline, the first section deals with judgment often recalling the past, the second section deals with hope frequently referring to the future, and the third section deals with the present and urges God's people to be reconciled to God. Therefore, we may suggest the following outline for the book:[9]

---

1) The Message of Destruction (1–3)
2) The Message of Restoration (4–5)
3) The Message of Reconciliation (6–7)

---

9. Like most scholars we prefer a three-part division of the material.

Micah

The purpose of the book is to point out that the destruction Israel and Judah are experiencing is the result of God's judgment upon sin. Covenant privileges do not provide immunity from God's judgment. However, the message of future restoration provides hope that encourages God's people to amend their lives. Therefore, readers are urgently exhorted, in light of past judgment and future hope, especially in the last section of the book, to be reconciled to God through repentance, faith, and righteous living.

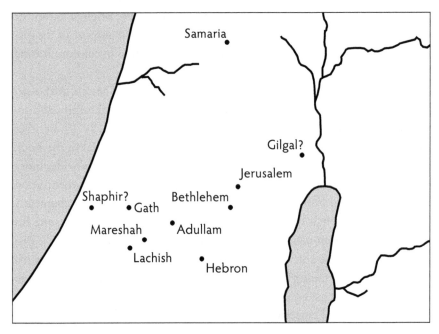

Figure 2. Map of Israel in the Eighth Century BC

INTRODUCTION

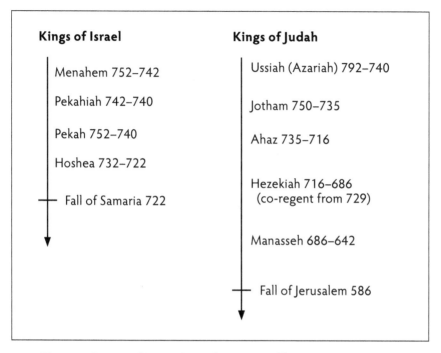

Figure 3. Reigns of Kings (note that reigns of kings are approximate and sometimes overlap due to rival kingdoms and co-regencies)

MICAH 1–3:
THE MESSAGE OF DESTRUCTION

MICAH 1

In the first three chapters of the book of Micah, the prophet points out that judgment and destruction are coming upon the world, because of the sin of God's people. The big problem with the world is not pagan wickedness but the idolatry of God's people, especially the sin of Israel's leaders, priests, and prophets. Micah's message of destruction would have been very confronting for the Israelites in the Old Testament. In the same way, Micah's message presents a big challenge for the church in Asia today.

1:1 An Urgent Call

The opening words of the book identify the prophet, the historical context, and the basic content of the book. Ancient literary works did not carry separate titles as modern books, and so the first sentence generally functioned as a "title." The structure of the heading here corresponds to the standard formula of four other books among the twelve minor prophets (Hos 1:1; Joel 1:1; Zeph 1:1; see also Amos 1:1), with minor variation, and reflects the hand of the final editor. It serves as an introduction to the whole book and provides the theological and historical framework for its interpretation.

The basic content or subject of the book concerns "the word of the LORD" (Mic 1:1). It is a standard expression taken from the tradition, first occurring in Genesis 15:1–4 where it relates to the covenant promise concerning the promised seed. The expression becomes prominent in the book of Exodus describing God's revelation to Moses. Later in the canon, "the word of the LORD" comes to denote the content of the prophetic message and is associated with the call of the prophet (see Isa 1:10; Jer 1:2, 4, 11, 13; Ezek 1:3; 3:16). In the Hebrew text "the word of the LORD" is emphatic standing at the head of the sentence and governs the whole book. Another possible translation of the term "word" is "message;" the book of Micah contains the message of the Lord for his people. The additional clause, "the vision he saw," provides further clarification of the content and nature of the message.[1] The "word" as not being heard but seen,

---

1. The Hebrew text reads "which he saw," the term "vision" is an interpolation by the NIV.

illustrates the impact of the message upon the prophet and reflects the poetic nature of the prophecy containing many pictorial images. Consequently, the word of the Lord is central and shapes the vision of the prophet. More specifically the content of the book concerns Samaria and Jerusalem, the capital cities of the northern and southern kingdoms respectively, which personify the people of God. The identification of the prophet as Micah of Moresheth, who prophesied during the days of Jotham, Ahaz, and Hezekiah, kings of Judah, provides important geographical and historical information for interpreting the prophecy. Apart from the book of Micah and the reference in Jeremiah 26:18, we do not know much about Micah. Apparently, judging from his location and the length of his prophecy, he was not as prominent as Isaiah or some of the other prophets in the canonical tradition who were located in Jerusalem. Nevertheless, even the people of lesser towns and the countryside needed a prophet. Indeed, they especially needed to hear the message since they would play a major role in God's plan of future restoration (see Mic 4:6–7; 5:2, 7–8). The name of the prophet Micah literally means, "Who is like Yahweh?" and is significant for understanding the main message of the book. At the end of the book the prophet specially asks, "Who is a God like you, who pardons sin and forgives the transgression of the remnant of his inheritance?" (Mic 7:18). As we will see, God will judge Israel, but amazingly out of this judgment rich mercy will flow through God's people to all nations. Although the message concerns Samaria and Jerusalem, only kings from Judah are listed. Perhaps, this observation indicates that while the message talks about Samaria, it especially concerns Jerusalem, since by the time the book of Micah appeared in its final form the northern kingdom was already destroyed and only Judah remained.

Our first point of application is to note that the expression "the word of the Lord" standing at the head of the prophecy reflects a fundamental characteristic of biblical faith. God's word, or the Bible, provides the foundation for Christian theology and life. Although historical events (God's intervention in history) undergird the truth-claims of the Christian faith, it is God's word that legitimizes and interprets the meaning of these historical events. Since the events are announced beforehand (i.e. predictive prophecy or fore-telling), we know that they did not happen by chance but by God's direct intervention in historical processes. And since God's word explains the meaning of the event, usually after it has happened, we have confidence about its significance for our lives. Thus, the general pattern of biblical revelation demonstrates the prominence of the Word.

Micah 1–3: The Message of Destruction

Therefore, teachers and pastors need to reflect on the important role of God's word in ministry. "The word of the LORD" calls the prophet into action and governs the prophet's ministry and message. Micah received the Lord's revelation (i.e. God's word). It is incumbent on every minister and teacher of the church to have a direct experience and first-hand knowledge of God's word. Asian Christians must be very grateful for the teaching and contribution of Western missionaries in the past. However, the church in Asia needs to mature, stand independently on its own feet, and develop its own contextualized theology. The only way to do that is for Asian Christians to study God's word for themselves. We may well ask, "Does the church value and emphasize the word of God?" Sadly, the Asian church has been influenced by the anti-intellectual tendency in some parts of the Western church today. People often quote 1 Corinthians 8:1, "knowledge puffs up," to undermine the serious study of God's word. However, in the context of 1 Corinthians, "knowledge" refers to things sacrificed to idols and not to the knowledge of God or it may even refer to one of the foolish slogans of the Corinthians that Paul opposes. In the Bible knowledge is highly valued (Ps 119:66; Prov 1:7; Isa 11:2, 9). Indeed, one reason for the demise of God's people is their rejection of knowledge (Isa 5:13; Hos 4:6). The Asian church needs to pay much more attention to theological education, to train the next generation of preachers.

We also note that Micah was from Moresheth, which was a small rural village. Although urbanization is happening fast in Asia, many people still live in rural areas. In China and Indonesia, 45 percent of the population still live in rural areas; it is 55 percent in the Philippines, 67 percent in India, and 82 percent in Nepal.[2] Rural Christians can be encouraged through the book of Micah because God's word not only addresses people in the city, where most wealth is accumulated and most decisions are made, but also rural farmers. As God is raising up preachers in the big cities, so too he is raising up many preachers from the rural areas of Asia. Rural Christians are by no means lesser citizens in God's kingdom. In fact, as we will see later in Micah's prophecy,

---

2. See *Rural Population* provided by The World Bank Group in 2016, estimates based on United Nations, World Urbanization Prospects (http://data.worldbank.org/indicator/SP.RUR.TOTL.ZS); and *World Urbanization Prospects United Nations 2014 Revision* (https://esa.un.org/unpd/wup/publications/files/wup2014-highlights.Pdf).

ordinary Christians have an important role to play in the fulfillment of God's plan of salvation.

1:2–7 The First Oracle of Judgment

The book of Micah opens with a graphic picture of global judgment on idolatry. The first two commands, "hear" and "listen," call all people of the world to attention. Even though the prophecy particularly concerns Samaria and Jerusalem it has worldwide implications. Everyone, including all the Gentile nations, must listen to the message of the prophet since God has been offended and will no longer remain passive. The expression that God is in "his holy temple" implies that God's holiness has been slighted. Verse 2 is similar to the opening of the book of Isaiah (Isa 1:2), where the heavens and the earth are called upon as witnesses against Israel. The message of Micah, however, is different: now the world comes under the judgment of God, not just Israel. The image of God coming out of his temple to judge is also reminiscent of the language of Isaiah (see Isa 6; 26:21).

Verse 3, providing the reason for the prophet's call, predicts impending judgment and destruction of all the high places. The command "look" has two levels of meaning: firstly, although the message is verbal, the pictorial language of the poetry paints a vivid picture that can be seen with the mind's eye; and secondly, the approaching judgment is not just metaphorical, but is about to happen in observable history. The expression "high places" is a technical term that refers to the temples of idolatry, usually built on hills, and to the idolatrous practices associated with them. Although these temples are built on hills, God is far above them and must "come down" to draw near to them. This call to the Gentiles and idolaters is the first of the four calls against God's enemies in section one of the book of Micah. Most Israelites would probably have endorsed the message of the prophet and would not have been particularly alarmed.

The next verse describes the result of God's judgment in poetic language (v. 4). The image of mountains melting before the Lord is a frequent image in biblical poetry and symbolizes the power of God's judgment (see Deut 32:22; Ps 68:2; Isa 42:15; 64:1; Nah 1:5). If mountains cannot stand before the Lord's presence, how much less human beings. As there is nothing intrinsic in water that can arrest its flow, so too all human structures and endeavors will simply disintegrate before God's judgment. The parallelism moving from high mountains to deep valleys forms a merismus (a figure of speech in which the whole is referred to by means of its parts) that includes all topography. Applied to humanity the comprehensive geographical image means that all levels of society will be affected by God's judgment, from lofty rulers to lowly peasants.

Verse 5 gives the reason for God's judgment; it is on account of the rebellion of Samaria and Jerusalem, i.e. the sin of God's people, that the whole world is judged. In other words, it appears that the prophet is holding the Israelites responsible for the idolatry of the Gentiles. Here, of course, one may imagine many objections to the prophet's message. Are the Gentile nations punished on account of Israel's transgression? Is that fair? What is the logic behind the prophetic message? In order to answer this question, we have to consider the wider canonical context of the prophetic message; the Israelites have responsibility for the world, since they are to be a light to the nations.

In the second half of verse 5 the prophet identifies the particular sin of Israel, viz. Samaria and Jerusalem, the respective capitals of the northern and southern kingdoms. In the following verses, the reason for mentioning the capital cities is explained. The rebellion of Samaria is idolatry and false worship. The books of 2 Kings and 1 Chronicles described the apostasy of the northern kingdom in detail. After Jeroboam II founded the northern kingdom he set up two golden calves at Bethel and Dan as alternative centers of worship to prevent his subjects to go to Jerusalem (1 Kgs 12:25–33). All subsequent Israelite kings "did what was evil in the eyes of the LORD" and "did not depart from the sins of Jeroboam." The idolatrous practices of Israel during the eighth century before the fall of Samaria in 722 BC are illustrated by the discovery of many clay figures of Canaanite divinities in Israelite settlements. According to verse 9, the sin of idolatry had also infected Jerusalem. Although, according to 2 Kings, Jotham (r. 740–736) "did what was right in the eyes of the LORD," he did not remove the high places (2 Kgs 15:34–35). His successor Ahaz (r. 736–716) was much worse and "and even sacrificed his son in the fire" (2 Kgs 16:3). He "also made idols for worshiping the Baals" (2 Chr 28:2), and copied the pagan worship of Damascus in Jerusalem (2 Kgs 16:10–19). Later in the book of Micah the sin of Jerusalem is also identified as corrupt leaders, priests, and prophets (Mic 3:10–12). However, the next king of Judah, Hezekiah, implemented much reform and "did what was right in the eyes of the LORD" (2 Kgs 18:3), by removing the high places and cleansing the temple of idolatrous practices.

Verses 6 and 7 describe the disaster that will fall on Samaria due to God's judgment on idolatry. Samaria was built by Omri, the most powerful king of Israel, on the Hill of Shemer, with strong fortification walls, which made the city very secure defensively (1 Kgs 16:24–28). However, the city of Samaria will become a ruin and will be used as a place for agriculture. The "pouring" of her stones into the valley echoes the figurative language of verse 4 where water pours down the slope. Whereas the judgment is pictured metaphorically in verse 4, it is described literally in verses 6 and 7. The city is going to be destroyed and will become a ruin; its idolatrous shrines will become a desolation (see Isa 1:7). The reason given for the destruction in the last line of verse 7 is that the city is built on income derived from profane practices. So too, the proceeds of her plundering will serve to foster pagan practices and worship. The cause for the destruction of Samaria is also outlined in 2 Kings 17:7–13, where the pagan idolatry of the Israelites is described. The final editor of the book of Kings appears to have been aware of prophets such as Micah who warned Israel. Archaeological excavations have unearthed the acropolis of the Israelite kings of Samaria and have yielded a large collection of figurines and ivories, illustrating the city's idolatry and luxurious living. According to Josephus, there was also a temple to Baal in Samaria.[3]

Figure 4. The cuneiform clay prism of Sargon II describes the fall of Samaria (Israel Museum)

This prophecy was fulfilled in the ninth year of the reign of Hoshea (c. 722 BC), when the city fell into Assyrian hands after a siege of three years (2 Kgs

---

3. In *The Antiquities of the Jews* (9:138). See William Whiston, *The Works of Josephus, Complete and Unabridged* (Peabody: Hendrickson, 1987), 254.

17:5–6). The Assyrian victory is inscribed on the clay prism of Sargon II which provides extra-biblical evidence, in addition to the city's archaeological ruins, for this historical event (see Figure 4). The Assyrian king exiled the northern tribes and brought other peoples from Persia to settle the land, who eventually became the Samaritans. After the oracle of chapter 1 Samaria disappears from the narrative, only Jerusalem remains. The implications are clear, Samaria has already been judged, and all hope for her is gone. Jerusalem, however, still stands, and may avert judgment if she repents. Past judgment upon Samaria serves as a graphic warning for present Jerusalem.

THE ROLE OF ISRAEL WITH RESPECT TO THE NATIONS

Understanding the canonical context of the prophets is crucial for discerning the message of the prophetic books. The history of Israel began with the calling of Abraham, in the framework of the Abrahamic covenant, to become the father of a new people. The Abrahamic covenant contained many promises and blessings, but its main goal, as described in Genesis, was that "all peoples on earth" would be blessed through Abraham and his descendants (Gen 12:3; 18:17–19; 22:18; 26:4; 28:14), which recalls God's initial intention for humanity before the fall (compare Gen 1:28). Abraham's descendants were to become a model of righteousness and so be a blessing to the surrounding nations (Gen 18:17–19). But, perhaps more importantly, the promised "seed" who would undo the work of the serpent would come from the line of Abraham (Gen 3:15; 4:25; 9:9; 12:7; 13:15–16; 15:3, 5, 13, 18; 17:7–10, 12, 19; see also Gal. 3:16). Already in the book of Genesis individuals and nations were blessed through Abraham's descendants (see Gen 30:27; 39:5; 47:7, 10). Later in the Mosaic covenant, which supplemented the Abrahamic covenant, Israel's role with respect to the nations became much more pronounced. Israel had to act as a witness to the Lord's uniqueness, righteousness, and mercy before the nations so that they too might come to honor the Lord and walk in his light. Therefore, the Lord's treatment of Israel was intended to demonstrate the Lord's glory in front of the nations (see Exod 14:4, 17–18; 19:5–6; Deut 4:6-8, 32-40; 7:7; 9:4-7; 10:12–22; see also 1 Pet 2:9); the Lord alone is God and there is no other. Evidently, God's intention was to partner with Israel to establish a new society of justice, holiness, and kindness that would be a light and a blessing to the nations. The role of Israel as a witness to the nations is also a major theme in the Psalms.[1] Unfortunately, however, according to the Old Testament account Israel did not fulfill this divine intention, but instead turned away from the Lord

> by worshiping idols and abandoning justice and mercy. Israel did not fulfill its role as a witness before the nations causing them to abandon idolatry, establish just societies, and worship the Lord alone. Therefore, Micah 1:5 indicates that Israel failed to carry out its mission to be a light to the Gentiles; idolatry and injustice are still rife among the nations. To be more exact, the Gentile nations are punished not on account of Israel's rebellion, but on account of their own transgressions; however, their continuous transgression shows up Israel's failure in being a model to influence the world for good. Therefore, Israel is indirectly responsible for the incessant and pervasive idolatry, leading to injustice, oppression, and all forms of immorality, present in the world.
>
> ---
>
> 1. For example, see Pss 2; 44; 47; 48; 68:28–35; 69:34–35; 72; 76; 82:8; 83:18; 89:14–15; 94:2; 96:3; 97:5; 98:9; 99; 105:1; 106:1–3; 107:8; 110:5–6; 114; 145; 147:2–3; 150; 156:7–9. See also Isa 43:10–12; 44:8; 55:4.

1:8–16 Lament over the Shame of God's People

In the following section, after the announcement of judgment upon Israel, there is a lament over the failure of God's people. But, the lament is not totally without hope, since the call to humiliation and repentance implies that change is possible. Where there is no hope, only despair and lethargy remain, but that is not the case here. We divided the lament, following the lead of Waltke, into three parts. Verses 8 to 9 introduce the lament, verses 10 to 15 describe the doom of Judah, and in the conclusion, verse 15, there is an urgent call to repentance while there is still time.[4]

1:8–9 The Prophet's Response

Micah's response to God's judgment upon his people is one of deep remorse and sadness. The heartfelt emotional language implies that judgment has already fallen upon Samaria; the northern kingdom is gone. The prophet is overcome with emotion. His reason for wailing is not because of the destruction of the idols and images, but rather because God's people have been overcome by idolatry and have failed to live up to their calling. Samaria's wound was incurable, she was not willing and able to change, and judgment and destruction were the inevitable result. The prophet's posture, going about "barefoot

---

4. Bruce K. Waltke, *Micah: An Introduction and Commentary*, TOTC (Leicester: InterVarsity Press, 1988), 153.

Micah 1–3: The Message of Destruction

and naked," reflects the custom of contrition at the time (see 2 Sam 15:30; Isa 20:2). Mourning was a communal or public affair, since the disaster has social consequences. Clothing was a symbol of one's status and honor; nakedness thus indicates a loss of status and honor.

Figure 5. The city gates of ancient Megiddo

But now, in addition, Samaria's sin has reached the gate of Jerusalem (v. 12). The southern kingdom, which is still standing, is in grave danger of experiencing the same judgment as its northern neighbor. Thus, we believe that by the time of the composition of the book, judgment had already fallen on Samaria, but Jerusalem was still the capital of the southern Davidic dynasty. The prophet understands Samaria's judgment as a portent of what will happen to Jerusalem unless the latter repents. Hence, Micah's lamentation is doubly loud, not just to mourn the end of Samaria, but also to serve as a warning to Jerusalem. The reference to "gate" is an allusion to the leadership of the city. Ancient city wall gates in Israel were constructed with a number of rooms or spaces where people could meet to conduct business and legal affairs (see Figure 5). In other words, the language indicates that the idolatry of Samaria has already infected the business, administrative, and legal affairs of the city of Jerusalem. Chinese often use the expression "the disease has attacked the vitals" (病入膏肓 *bing ru gao huang*) to describe a hopeless situation. There is not much the doctor can do for the patient. The Hebrew expression that the sin of Samaria "has reached the very gate of my people" carries a similar nuance; there is not much hope for Judah. Micah hopes that the people will understand the seriousness of their situation.

This section describes Micah's response to the coming judgment of God. He is deeply affected, goes about barefoot and naked, and mourns like jackals and ostriches. Several reasons lie behind the prophet's strong emotional reaction to God's judgment. Firstly, since he loves God's people and has great concern for them, he is very sad to see their ruin. He feels their distress and suffers with them.

Today we, as the servants of God, are to be like Micah and enter into the experience of the church and society when they suffer. Micah did not gloat over their plight, saying "I told you so." No, instead he was overcome with grief. He knew that the judgment upon Samaria would also affect Judah and his own village. No church is an island.

Secondly, since Israel failed to be a witness, Micah was overcome with shame and regret. Israel was supposed to be a witness to the nations of God's holiness, righteousness, justice, and compassion, instead Israel became exactly like the other nations. In some respects, Israel was even worse than the Gentile nations because of her hypocrisy and arrogance. What a great shame! What a great dishonor! What a great humiliation! And what's more, now that Israel had failed so miserably, God's great plan in the Abrahamic covenant that all nations should be blessed through Israel lay in ruins. What a pity for both Israel and the world! We see the same disappointment in the Lord Jesus when he wept over Jerusalem (Luke 19:41–44). How do we respond to the failures of the church and God's people in the world? Do we recognize that we are part of the church and have a responsibility? Are we saddened to tears when we see the failures of the church, especially when the church's failures are paraded before society? Or, are we unaffected as long as we can continue to live comfortable and secure lives? How great a concern do we have for God's kingdom and his reputation in the world? Or, are we like King Hezekiah who when he heard about the coming judgment of the Babylonian exile was unaffected because it would not happen in his lifetime? (see Isa 39:5–8). What a regrettable attitude in the heart of the king of God's people!

And, thirdly, Micah's emotional response is to express repentance and to encourage others to do the same. God's judgment is about to come, but there is still a glimmer of hope. It is not too late.

Micah 1–3: The Message of Destruction

1:10–15 Lamentation over the Cities of Judah

The main portion of the lamentation relates to the impending doom of the southern kingdom. Micah describes the destiny of several Judean towns; all of them lie within a 15-kilometer radius of the prophet's hometown of Moresheth (see Figure 2). The location of most of the towns mentioned here is known by archaeologists today, but a few remain uncertain. Even though Jerusalem is the focus of the prophetic address, all of Judah will be affected by the coming judgment. The general population will not escape the grave consequences of Jerusalem's fall. Hence, the prophet has a message for those who live around him some distance removed from the nation's capital. The matters addressed in the prophecy concerns all the people of God and not just the leaders in Jerusalem. A list of ten towns, five mentioned before Jerusalem and five after, may be deliberate to indicate the totality of God's people. The number ten is often used in the Bible to indicate completeness (e.g. Ten Commandments).

Although several exegetes have attempted to provide a symmetric and a consistent pattern of meter in the lamentation, all attempts are less than convincing. Perhaps, the inconsistent poetic meter reflects the chaotic result of judgment and exile. All meaningful patterns and regularity break down into despair and consternation under God's judgment. Rather, the main literary feature of the section is an abundance of puns and word plays based on the names of the towns. The function of these word plays is to create a deep impression upon the memory of the hearers and to spur them on to appropriate action. The prophet's lamentation is memorable and finely tuned, which would have undoubtedly made a deep impression on the hearers. These word plays do not have any intrinsic theological significance in the terms themselves, but serve to create a memorable impression on the minds of the hearers.[5] The main function of these puns is to underscore the nation's incurable disease; it is almost as if her identity is bound up with rebellion and defeat. How can she be healed and escape? The language describes the defeat and exile of Judah as a present reality to emphasize the imminent danger of their situation.

The exclamation "tell it not in Gath" (v. 10), a Philistine city, does not mean that Gath will not know about the disaster that will befall Judah, but rather expresses the prophet's sadness over the shame that will be due to God's

---

5. H. W. Wolf has provided a creative translation to illustrate the effect of the word plays for the modern reader: "In Dustville roll yourselves in the dust . . . Portland will lose its port . . . 'No Parking' will be the sign plastered on Parkland . . . The place called Victoria will henceforth be called the Place of Defeat . . .". In *Micah the Prophet*, translated by Ralph D. Gehrke (Philadelphia: Fortress, 1981), 40–41.

people in the eyes of their enemies. Micah wants the shame of Israel to be contained. They should not hang out their dirty washing for all to see, so to speak. The language recalls David's lament for Saul and Jonathan after their demise (2 Sam 1:20). Micah's injunction imitates that of David, Israel's most ideal king. The news should not be proclaimed in Gath, lest the Gentiles rejoice over the failure and defeat of Israel's royal family. It is interesting to note that the final town or region in the list, Adullam, also recalls the experience of David when he fled from the king of Gath (1 Sam 22:1). Therefore, the juxtaposition of Gath and Adullam evokes a tradition of Israel's failure and weakness with respect to her enemies and form a kind of *inclusio* for the whole section. Gath and Adullam are associated with the shame of Israel's monarchy.

Figure 6. The Assyrian Siege of Lachish in 701 BC as depicted on the wall of the Assyrian Palace (Israel Museum). Original in the British Museum.

The most well-known Judean town mentioned in the list, apart from Jerusalem, is Lachish (v. 13). It was one of the most fortified cities of the region and served to protect the western advance to Jerusalem. The city was besieged and most probably captured by Sannacherib in 701 BC when King Hezekiah revolted against Assyrian influence in the region (see 2 Kgs 18:13–17; 19:8; Isa 36:2). Archaeological excavations have revealed the siege ramp the Assyrians used to attack the city. The siege of Lachish also features prominently on the large alabaster slabs that decorated the walls of the royal palace in Nineveh.

The original reliefs are now housed in the British Museum (see Figure 6). Micah singles out Lachish as the beginning of Zion's sin, which most probably reflects Judah's reliance on military means and political alliances for protection.

The conqueror envisaged in verse 15 may refer in the first instance to the Assyrians who raided many Judean towns in the reign of Hezekiah, but then especially to the Babylonian campaign around a hundred years later at the beginning of the sixth century, which led to the exile of the southern kingdom. The glory of Israel refers to the flight of the Davidic king, and may either be understood in a literal sense, that the Judean king will in fact flee to the same region as David did, or as a figurative description of the downfall of the Davidic monarchy which occurred under the Babylonian exile.

1:16 Final Judgment of Exile

Following on from his own experience and example, the prophet calls on all God's people to humble themselves with the ritual practice of contrition. The reason for contrition and shame is exile. In itself exile is not an experience that necessarily calls for humility and repentance. Rather, the reason of Israel's destruction, humiliation, and exile is because she departed from the ways of the Lord. The reason for Israel's demise is not the power of Assyria, but the evil of Israel's own idolatry. The last line, "for they will go from you into exile," forms the climax of the section and can be regarded as a predictive prophecy. It can also be translated, "for they have gone into exile," indicating the present reality. Most probably, during the time of the original readers, Samaria has already fallen into the hands of the Assyrians (722 BC). In other words, many of the early prophetic announcements of the prophet have already been fulfilled. It is this perspective, the fulfillment of previously announced judgment that sets the tone of the entire book. Jerusalem and the southern kingdom still stand, but the same threat of judgment hangs over them. The fulfillment of early prophecies concerning Samaria, thus, serves as a stark and urgent warning to the people who were still living in the southern kingdom. The words "from you" refer to people or the remnant who will remain in the land after the exile. The prophetic word is not a vain threat. Again, covenant privileges do not make one immune from God's judgment. In the words of Smith, "We cannot accept God's love and reject his lordship."[6] Indeed, judgment will begin with the house of Israel.

---

6. Ralph L. Smith, *Micah-Malachi*, WBC, Vol. 32 (Dallas, Texas: Word Books, 1984), 35.

Micah

Micah's lamentation is a good illustration of the complexity and multifaceted nature of biblical prophecy. The poetry has been crafted through a rich intermingling of new prophetic insight, historical experience (which in this case was the fall of Samaria), previous literary traditions, as well as future hope. It does include the aspect of predictive prophecy, which may have multiple fulfillments, but most importantly it contains proclamation that reveals God, who he is and what he does, and urges appropriate action. The main point of the prophecy is that God abhors the idolatry of his people and will bring judgment and disaster upon them because of their sins unless they repent.

In 1 Timothy 2:1–6, Paul urges us to pray for all people, for kings and for rulers, because God desires all people to be saved and to come to the knowledge of the truth. As Asian Christians, we need to pray for our nation and compatriots that God may give them a heart of repentance and faith. Just like Psalm 33:12 says, "Blessed is the nation whose God is the Lord, the people he chose for his inheritance." If a nation has no faith, it also has no hope and future. There is a Chinese proverb that says, "Everyone is responsible for his country" (天下兴亡，匹夫有责 *tian xiaxing wang, pi fu you ze*). We should not think that God's judgment on ancient Israel and other nations has nothing to do with us, since God is the creator of all and "watches all who live on earth" (Ps 33:14). He made us, sustains us, and also observes our behavior. Therefore, every Christian, every country, and every people group will give an account to God for their behavior. The way of escape is also with God as King David affirms, "The Lord is close to the brokenhearted and saves those who are crushed in spirit" (Ps 34:18).

IMPENDING JUDGMENT UPON THE CHURCH

The message of these verses is alarming. God is coming to judge the world because of idolatry. The prophet does not just address the church, but the world at large. According to the Bible, God is the creator and sustainer of all humanity and expects that all humanity worship him exclusively. He will judge idolatry, injustice, greed, exploitation, and immorality. In fact, this biblical conviction that God is the ultimate ruler and that all governments are responsible to him is also very deeply rooted in Chinese tradition. Ancient Chinese believed that the emperor governs under the "Mandate of Heaven" (天命 *tian ming*) and that Heaven (or God) will remove bad rulers. History, both East and West, are full of examples that this is indeed the case.

This is a provocative message for Asia, but it must be proclaimed publicly. Asia has undergone tremendous development over the last few decades. Literacy, educational levels, and technological know-how have risen considerably. There also has been much growth in economic wealth and political power to the extent that Asia is fast becoming the hub of global affairs. However, at the same time Asia is still rife with the idolatry and superstition of its traditional religions. The new obsession with economic development has also led to much exploitation of people and the environment. There are unprecedented levels of greed and corruption at every level of society. The stark prophetic message is that God is going to judge idolatry and immorality. In fact, it appears that Asia is already experiencing a growing number of disasters: earthquakes, tsunamis, aircraft calamities, epidemics, terrorist attacks, and economic instability. Could there be a theological reason behind these disasters? Are these warning signs of greater catastrophes to come? It is the task of the preacher and the church to warn society about God's impending judgment.

But there is even a harsher message for the church. According to verse 5, it is on account of the sins of God's people that the world is going to be judged. As God intended Israel to be a blessing to the nations, the church is to be salt and light to the world (Matt 5:13–16). The church already has had a long presence in many Asian countries and has grown deep indigenous roots. However, has the Asian church recognized its responsibility towards society? It appears that sometimes the church lives in a kind of Christian enclave detached from society or unwilling to engage with current issues. The witness and prophetic voice of the church have often been very faint. Instead, other voices and ideologies, which have been in Asia for a much shorter time, have gained the upper hand. For example, the rise of communism in the twentieth century in many parts of Asia happened almost overnight. Today, materialism, militarism, consumerism, and hedonism are the driving ideologies behind many Asian societies. These ungodly "isms" have already caused much havoc and suffering for Asians. One may think of the misery triggered by the Cultural Revolution in China and the despair produced by the exploitation of the environment in many parts of Southeast Asia. Could the church in some measure be responsible for this suffering, having failed to provide a prophetic voice and a better vision for life? Micah is holding Israel responsible for the idolatry of the surrounding nations, and as the surrounding nations will be judged, the judgment will begin with the people of God. Again, in the example of the Cultural Revolution, Christians suffered greatly. One may well reflect whether we may see the judging hand of God in these events. Micah's message is that God may well hold the church responsible for the state of society. The church has a priestly function within the world; it exists to be a mediator between humanity and God. God wants to use the church to change society, but if the church loses its saltiness it will be discarded (see Luke 14:34–35; Rev 2:5). Therefore, the church must resist the temptation to retreat, like the Chinese literati retreated to the mountains whenever the nation was overpowered by foreign rulers.

The message of Micah calls Christians to examine themselves. Do we entertain "idols" in our hearts? Do we substitute Jesus for other things? Are we exalting some theological or philosophical tradition above the word of God? Are we just like the world? In his book *Counterfeit Gods* (2009), Timothy Keller has identified many idols that Western Christians pursue today, including money, sex, success, security, and power. Many Western Christians are exactly the same as their non-Christian neighbors. Are we in Asia any different? We know that many historical churches in the West have been greatly influenced by liberal theology and are more or less empty today. Since they have departed from God's word, they have lost credibility, relevance, and the ability to transform society. Their lampstand has been taken away (Rev 2:5). Many church denominations in the West have already recognized homosexual marriage and have ordained practicing homosexuals as ministers. Obviously, these churches have deviated from the moral standard and teaching of the Bible. In addition, in today's pulpit, many ministers do not preach the gospel anymore, but instead proclaim prosperity theology or the ideology of positive thinking. The Bible's teaching on sin, judgment, repentance, faith, and salvation in Jesus Christ are seldom mentioned. The sad result is that the church in the West is losing ground and Western society is becoming increasingly pagan again. All of this should serve as a warning to the church in Asia. We should not deviate from the word of God to pursue idols, because God will judge sin and idolatry. When the book of Micah was written, Samaria was already judged and destroyed. The same judgment will fall on Jerusalem, the southern kingdom, unless she repents and turns back to God. In Asia today we should avoid blindly following the church in the West, aping the trends of secular society.

MICAH 1–3: THE MESSAGE OF DESTRUCTION

MICAH 2

With the oracles of judgment in chapters 2 and 3, the prophet becomes much more explicit about the identity of the sinners and the nature of their sins. The message of judgment is more and more threatening as it centers on the rich, the powerful and spiritual elite of the nation. In chapter 1, the prophet commences his message with judgment upon the Gentile nations and Israel in general. However, in chapters 2 and 3 he is much more specific; judgment now falls on the rich landowners of Israel, the leaders of God's people, and finally even upon the prophets themselves. There is an intensification in the disconsolate mood of the prophecy as judgment moves from the Gentiles to the people of God, and eventually to the civil and religious leaders of Israel. One may well imagine that most Israelites would have agreed, saying "amen" to the announcement of judgment upon the Gentiles in chapter 1, much like the prophet Jonah desired judgment to fall on the Ninevites. And when the judgment of destruction moves to the sinners of Israel – the unjust landowners – many Israelites probably would not have objected to the message. But the judgment does not stop there; it moves on and singles out the civil leaders, the priests, and the prophets as the targets of God's wrath. It is a comprehensive and very confrontational proclamation of judgment upon all levels of society. No one is without excuse and everyone stands under condemnation.

2:1–5 Judgment upon Sinners

The oracle of doom is introduced with the word "woe" (*hôy*), whose original setting stems from funeral processions (1 Kgs 13:30; Jer 22:18; see also Amos 6:1–11). In the prophets, the use of the word often indicates both accusation and threat (see Isa 1:4; Amos 5:16; 6:1–7), but in a few contexts, it is simply used as an exclamation to take note (Isa 55:1; Zech 2:6–7). The word is used only once in Micah as an indictment against "sinners," i.e. the rich who are exploiting the poor. "Woe" is pronounced over them. In fact, Micah is announcing their funeral! The "sinners" are described as those who "plan iniquity" and who "carry it out." The poetic parallelism pictures an escalation in their evil behavior and an intensification of their greed. They first think about doing evil and then they actually go ahead and do it. Every night, when they should be resting and meditating on God's word (Pss 1:2; 4:4; 36:4; 149:5), they think up schemes to defraud people out of their property and means of living. Ironically, but also very sadly, they do evil at the first sight of morning light. Petty thieves commit their crimes at night, but powerful tyrants commit theirs in broad daylight. They have no fear of punishment and no one dares to confront them or bring them to account. Or, perhaps, their evil behavior is accepted by society because it has become the norm. Their avarice is all the more heinous because they have no need to increase their wealth; they do it simply because they have the power to do so.

The expression "their inheritance" (v. 2) recalls the history and labor of a person's forbearers and has covenantal connotations (see Deut 12:9). One's "inheritance" is not only received by the right of succession, but is also the promised gift that God has allotted to the children of Israel. It is received as a covenantal blessing from the Lord and provides each individual with status, sustenance, and security. Indeed, one of the central covenant blessings consisted in the giving of land to the people of God. In the ancient world, land meant security, identity, and provided a means of living. According to Alfaro, "It was through the possession of a parcel of land that the individual Israelite was to enjoy liberty, dignity, and sufficiency."[7] Hillers states that, "each under his own vine and his own fig tree summarizes the ideal."[8] Therefore, one of the biggest misadventures a person could face was the loss of land, since it often led to oppression and slavery. There were many stipulations within the Mosaic law that served to protect the individual's right to land and to prevent loss of inheritance (see Lev 25:10–34; Deut 19:14; 27:17).

The fraudulent landowners have no moral or spiritual restraint; they have become totally insensitive to human need as well as to spiritual values. The many copulas ("and") in verse 2 is unusual in Hebrew poetry; the author probably inserted them to evoke a sense of unceasing exploitation. The wealthy go beyond all limits and they never stop amassing wealth at the expense of ordinary people. The root cause for their actions is covetousness and greed. Just as Adam and Eve coveted the forbidden fruit (Gen 3:6), so they covet that which does not belong to them. The tenth commandment specifically states, "You shall not set your desire on your neighbor's house or land" (Deut 5:21; Exod 20:17). It is worth mentioning here that Moresheth is located on the Shephelah, the lower hill country between the coastal plains and the hills of Judea, which is prime agricultural land. The flat and fertile lots of the small farmers must have been very tempting for the greedy. According to the Torah, the covenant community should be characterized by honesty,

---

7. Juan I. Alfaro, *Justice and Loyalty: A Commentary on the Book of Micah* (Grand Rapids, MI: Eerdmans, 1989), 22.
8. Delbert R. Hillers, *Micah: A Commentary on the Book of the Prophet Micah* (Philadelphia: Fortress, 1988), 33.

righteousness, and mercy. Instead, the land grabbers have sinned against God and their neighbors.

In 2 Kings 15:10–22 there are several examples of the trickery and violence Micah is denouncing. Around 750 BC, Shallum led a conspiracy and assassinated King Zechariah, only to be supplanted in turn by the military general Menahem one month later. Menahem became notorious for ripping open the pregnant women of the city of Tiphsah and for pillaging silver from the ordinary folk of the land to pay off the Assyrian king to secure his own position. Such behavior among the leaders shows that they had no concern for the welfare of ordinary people, but cared only for themselves. Consequently, since they are planning adversity against their neighbors, God is planning adversity against them. The same word for their "planning" and God's "planning" is used in the Hebrew text; they are reaping what they have sown. Distressingly, because of their sins, God is planning to judge and destroy his own people (see Isa 45:7).

The word "people" in verse 3 denotes a "clan" or "family," and probably refers to the class of rich landowners, indicating that they have formed a clique, like the Mafia, to advance their selfish interests. In the Hebrew text, there is also an exclamation "behold" which indicates that disaster is about to fall on them. A time of adversity is coming which will humiliate and shame them. Specifically, the adversity will involve a loss of land; that which they coveted the most will be taken away. The expression "from which you cannot save yourself" literally reads, "you will not be able to remove your necks" and means that there will be no escape from God's judgment. In the ancient world captives were tightly bound by ropes around their necks, which made any struggle or attempt to run away just a quicker way to death (see Isa 3:16; Jer 27:12; Lam 5:5).

Verse 4 describes the lamentation that many Israelites will take up. "In that day" is a common expression in the Hebrew Bible, occurring 208 times, and ordinarily refers to the imminent coming of the event being narrated. However, in the Prophets it becomes eschatological, i.e. it refers to an indeterminate time in the future in which the prophecy will be fulfilled. The translation, "they will taunt you with this mournful song" (NIV) or "they will take up a lament against you" (NASB), implies that Israel's enemies are taunting them. However, in the Hebrew text the preposition *'al* translated as "against" also means "about" or "concerning"; it does not necessarily imply animosity (i.e. "against") (see Gen 31:17; 42:26; Jer 3:2). It is better to understand the singers to be the Israelites. A person will compose a lament about the coming destruction. The Hebrew verbs are in the singular to highlight personal cost and individual grief, but in the Hebrew text the lament itself is sung with the plural pronoun "we" because the desolation will be a communal experience. The lament envisages a process of dispossession or a gradual decline, which makes the adversity much worse. Their land and possessions will slowly but surely disappear from their grasp, and they will be powerless to arrest the reduction of their territory. This was indeed what happened during the invasion of the Assyrians into Israel starting from Tiglath-Pileser's first campaign in 745 BC (see 2 Kgs 15:29; 16:5–16) with intermittent incursions into the land, followed by the annexation of cities, until the eventual fall of Samaria in 722 BC. But, more importantly, the process of judgment culminates with the loss of the blessing of the covenant in the assembly of the Lord. It is not just that they will lose their land; they will lose their place or status in the covenant community. There will be a dramatic reversal of fortunes. "They will learn that history is not the product of human or blind forces, but that it is in the power of God which will cause things to happen."[9] Finally, it is noteworthy to point out that verse 5 assumes, that even after the disaster of the exile, the assembly of the Lord will continue to exist.

---

9. Alfaro, *Justice and Loyalty: A Commentary on the Book of Micah*, 25.

MICAH 1–3: THE MESSAGE OF DESTRUCTION

INJUSTICES WITHIN THE CHURCH TODAY

It is important to note two key points for today. Firstly, in the prophecy of Micah the judgment of destruction described in chapter 2 is coming upon Israel or the people of God. It is not talking about the sin and condemnation of the Gentiles or those who do not know God; rather it is exclusively dealing with the covenant people. Secondly, we also need to note the nature of the sin that is renounced by the prophet. It is not immorality or impiety that is being condemned, but the exploitation of others. The prophet severely condemns the evils of injustice, unkindness, and avarice.

Micah's message to the Israelites is as relevant today as it was then. God's intention for his people to be a community of righteousness and a light for the nations, and his abhorrence of exploitation and injustice, have not changed. In the same way, as judgment fell upon Samaria reducing it to a pile of rubble, so too God's judgment will fall upon exploitation and injustice in the church. Exploitation of the poor, or social sin, is rife in many Asian societies, but unfortunately, sometimes also in the Asian church. Like the West, Asian society has been mesmerized and subjugated by the idol of economic growth and prosperity, and this idol is also influencing the worldview and value system of many Asian Christians. The ultimate criterion of behavior has become personal gain, not the values of God's kingdom. Many in society use their position to exploit others for personal gain. This also happens in the church. For many, the church has become just another "industry" to be exploited for one's own personal agenda of prosperity and power. A recent example of such behavior is the jailing of the leaders of Singapore's City Harvest Church for misappropriating church funds (US$35 million) to support the singing career of the senior pastor's wife. The judge found that the church leaders misused the trust of the congregation, falsified accounts, and committed many criminal breaches. City Harvest Church emulates the mega-church models from the US that entice believers with slick worship services and a "prosperity gospel." The message links prosperity with Christianity and measures "spirituality" in terms of stunning looks, personal success, status, and wealth.

But the abuse of God's people by church leaders does not just occur in big mega-churches. In some Asian countries many churches have a hierarchical leadership structure without any oversight or accountability, resulting in the spiritual abuse of the members. Spiritual abuse of others for selfish interests can have devastating effects upon victims, such as anxiety, low self-esteem, depression, disillusionment, break in relationships, and even ill-health. The person in power uses "spiritual" means to control, manipulate, and restrict the freedom of others. They tend to be authoritarian and legalistic, and any criticism is deemed to be a sign of disobedience to God or some other form of sin. Some church leaders hide the church's finances from the congregation

> and expel those who want more transparency, even accusing them of heresy. Ordinary believers often experience hurt. A few years ago, an Indian missionary in Tamil Nadu abducted young Buddhist girls from Nepal and portrayed them as orphans of murdered Christians in order to raise funds from Western churches. The fraud and exploitation went on for over a decade until the children were rescued from the orphanage by an anti-trafficking charity. It is heart-wrenching to hear such stories, and it is abominable that this exploitation and deceit were carried out by so-called Christians.
>
> As God used the Assyrians and Babylonians to judge Israel, so too God often uses the world, the secular judicial system in the examples cited above, to judge the church. Not only will these leaders who misuse and exploit God's people lose their social and economic standing, they will also lose their place within the community of believers (see Rev 3:5). When we do not appreciate and treasure the heritage that God has given to us, God will take it away and give it to others. Wealthy Christians and church leaders need to pay careful attention to Micah's warnings. Those who exploit God's people for their own personal advantage, however spiritual or successful they may seem, will be judged.

2:6–11 Objection by the People and the Response by the Prophet

This section records the response of the rich and fraudulent landowners to the message of Micah. Instead of recognizing their sin and repenting, they try to silence the voice of the prophet. They demand that the prophets do not preach about judgment and disaster, instead they want to hear messages of comfort and of good things to come.[10] They find it hard to accept that God can be angry with his people and that disaster is coming upon the land. Israel experienced much prosperity and even expanded her territory during the first half of the eighth century. How could anyone doubt that God's favor was upon his people? They probably thought that the increasing incursions of the Assyrian army into the land of Israel were just minor challenges to the security of the nation and could be controlled. After all, they were the covenant people and God would not abandon them. In other words, the rich had many social and theological

---

10. It is interesting to note the plural command. Micah was not alone in condemning the evil practices of the rich and powerful. We know that his ministry was contemporaneous or overlapped with Amos, Hosea, and Isaiah. Amos had a similar experience when Amaziah tried to silence his preaching (see Amos 7:10–13).

MICAH 1–3: THE MESSAGE OF DESTRUCTION

reasons to object to Micah's message of doom. They were not irreligious or hostile to the prophets, they were just against anyone who denounced their behavior and business practices. In verse 7 we see that they doubted that God was angry with them, or that God had brought adversity to the land. They thought that God would not become angry or bring disaster upon them.

However, the prophet responds with the words of the Lord. God's people have become his enemy, since by their behavior of exploiting the poor they oppose God's plan to establish a society of justice, compassion, and peace. The greedy landowners are the real enemies of God, not the Assyrians! They defraud women and children, those who cannot defend themselves (see Deut 27:19). Micah's message is more forceful than Isaiah's in denouncing the rich, perhaps because in the countryside he has first-hand observation and experience of their crimes.

An interesting pre-exilic letter came to light that provides first-hand evidence of the situation that the text is addressing in verse 8, "you strip off the rich robe from those who pass by without a care" (NIV), or perhaps more accurately "you strip off the mantle from those passing by in peace."

Figure 7. Ancient Hebrew letter (Israel Museum)

In the letter, which was written by a scribe on an ostracon (potsherd), a farm laborer appeals to a judge to have his garment returned to him. It appears that his garment had been seized by a landowner on the pretext that the laborer did not fulfill his contract. The letter reads:

> Let my lord the Governor pay heed to the words of his servant.
> Several days ago, your servant was harvesting in Hasar-asam.

> The work went as usual and your servant completed the harvesting and storing of my quota of grain . . . Despite the fact that your servant had completed his assigned work, Hoshaiahu, son of Shobai, kept your servant's cloak. He has held my cloak for days. All my fellow workers will testify, all those who work in the heat of the day will surely certify, that I am not guilty of any breach of contract. Please order my supervisor to return my cloak either in fulfillment of the law or as an act of mercy. Please do not remain silent, and leave your servant without his cloak.[11]

In the many repetitions we can hear the desperation of the poor laborer and the urgency of the situation. Exodus 22:26–27 specifically addresses the requirement not to withhold essential needs from the poor. Micah as a scribe may have written letters such as this to appeal to governors about the exploitation of the poor. Therefore, the "robe" in Micah 2:8 may not just be a figurative indication of status, but is probably referring to what really happened in the physical exploitation of the poor.

Figure 8. Remnants of Hezekiah's broad wall in Jerusalem

---

11. Victor H. Matthews and Don C. Benjamin, *Old Testament Parallels: Laws and Stories from the Ancient Near East*, Newly Revised and Expanded Third Edition (Mahwah, NJ: Paulist Press, 1997), 306.

Micah 1–3: The Message of Destruction

The words of verses 10 to 11 may be addressed either to those facing judgment, or to the faithful remnant, especially if the words form a unit with the promise of verses 12 and 13. If we prefer the former interpretation, the commands "Get up, go away" (or "arise and go") are sarcastically directed against evil-doers. They are about to leave the land and go into exile. The land has ceased to be the land of promise (Deut 12:10). Instead, they are destroying it because of injustice and inhumanity. Ironically, then, the landowners are going to be evicted as well. It is also possible to translate the last line of verse 10 as, "Because of uncleanness, you are destroying (*the land/people*) with a grievous destruction." Another interpretation, which is preferred by most translations and commentators, is to understand the verses as being addressed to the faithful. In this case, the commands "get up, go away (arise and go)" exhort the faithful to escape the destruction before it happens. Perhaps, the prophet is advising them to move to the southern kingdom of Judah. We know from archaeological excavations that Jerusalem expanded significantly in size during the reign of Hezekiah (c. 729–686), which required the construction of a second city wall (see Figure 8). Such an injunction also reminds us of Jesus' advice to the Christians of Jerusalem to flee the city before its destruction by the Romans in 70 AD (see Mark 13:14–18; Matt 24:15–20). In any case, the faithful remnant is free to leave and escape the land of Israel, since there is no hope for the nation. Israel is no longer willing to receive correction and amend her ways. Rather, Israel prefers lies and deceit. Even the prophets have become corrupted. The words "I will prophesy for you plenty of wine and beer" (literally, "preaching to you *of* wine and strong drink") indicate that they preach in a way that soothe the consciences of evil-doers in order to avoid tension and hostility from the powerful. Or, another way to understand verse 11 is that they are "preaching to you *for* wine and strong drink" (i.e. for personal gain). In light of Micah 3:5 this latter rendering is to be preferred. These preachers are not interested in the truth of the word of the LORD, but only consider their own comfort by avoiding hostility and chasing luxury. Despite the gravity of the situation, the rich land grabbers still prefer lies and preachers with soothing words. It is important to note that the target of Micah's condemnation is the rich landowners; it is only in chapter 3 that the prophet is addressing the priests and prophets. He is slowly narrowing his aim as he moves along. In chapter 2 there is no condemnation of the preachers yet; the rich landowners are criticizing the preachers who disapprove their actions.

WORLDLY VALUES AMONG CHRISTIANS

How do we respond to Micah's condemnation of the wicked landowners? All of us, probably, would apply the message to others who are notorious for their crimes. It does not often occur to us that we may be the real targets of Micah's piercing criticism. The rich landowners had many reasons for thinking that they were not under condemnation but enjoyed God's approval, and that Micah's message was misdirected. Was their prosperity not a sign of God's favor and blessing? Often, we do not perceive that we have totally imbibed the contemporary idols of secular society and that our real values are no different from unbelievers around us. The idols of our consumerist and commercial culture have become ours too. There is no perceptible difference in the behavior and lifestyles of Christians and non-Christians; we have the same morals, maintain the same houses, and pursue the same goals. Paul calls greed idolatry (Col 3:5) and warns that those who desire to be rich will suffer much pain (1 Tim 6:6–10). There is not much preaching today on the dangers of pursuing wealth or worldly power, nor much condemnation of covetousness. The pursuit of prosperity has become the "new normal."

It appears that many Asian churches have completely swallowed the intoxicating cocktail of Western Christendom which so easily attaches the Christian label to everything that the flesh and heathendom esteem. Instead of changing the world and its values, Western Christendom has "Christianized" the pursuits of heathendom by approving sensual pleasures, material goods, and worldly titles and decorations. Journalist Aries C. Rufo with his book, *Altar of Secrets: Sex, Politics, and Money in the Philippine Catholic Church*, published in 2013, has exposed systemic corruption, greed, misconduct, and exploitation of the vulnerable among bishops and priests. It reminds one of the corruption in the Catholic Church during the Dark Middle Ages. In Protestantism, too, the mega-churches of the West with their glitzy services, polished performances, and programs that meet every imaginable consumer need, have become the new models to follow. The New Testament message of self-denial and cross-bearing, repentance and faith, the scandal of a rejected and crucified Messiah, has been replaced with a message that does not offend, that does not challenge, and that does not change the world. Whereas the New Testament encourages humility, chastity, poverty, and honesty for the sake of the gospel, the "new normal" endorses arrogance, lewdness, riches, and hypocrisy. The church, which is supposed to possess the truth, in reality, perverts it. Christian leaders do their best to be seen with celebrities, politicians, and the rich. Christians, and especially Christian leaders, no longer perceive that there is a big contradiction between their lives and the teachings of Jesus and Paul in the New Testament. Instead of changing the world and its values, the world is changing the church and its theology.

> In light of Micah's message, the greatest danger to the future of the church in Asia is not some anti-Christian totalitarian government, but the worldly values and behavior of Christian leaders and pastors. God's greatest enemy does not stand outside the church, but is present within it. One thing is sure, the Christian label will not protect Christian leaders and churches against God's judgment. God will judge ungodly behavior in the church just as much as he will condemn it in the world. Therefore, we cannot expect to have a claim on God's protection and blessing, when our actions consistently deny him. People do not like to listen to messages that expose sin and threaten judgment, rather they like to be comforted and encouraged in their self-centered pursuits. When pastors preach against worldly behavior, instead of repenting, worldly Christians often simply stop coming to church. Pastors who want to gain favor have their own "theologies," which are superimposed upon the Bible, designed to be attractive. Many pulpits have become megaphones for entertainment and positive thinking, rather than a trumpet of salvation from the Lord. But true servants of God, according to the example of Micah, will be faithful to the biblical message and will not cease to preach the gospel because their message is unpopular. The prophet's recommendation to Christians who find themselves in churches with leaders that exploit ordinary believers and espouse worldly values is for them to leave.

2:12–13 Oracle of Salvation

Amidst oracles of doom and judgment there is a word of hope and salvation. Due to the failure of Israel, the people of God will be scattered and go into exile, fulfilling the prophecies of Deuteronomy. However, those who yearn for righteousness and God's salvation are not left without hope. Through the words of the prophet, God assures his faithful ones that he will again gather them together. They will find a haven of rest and will become a beacon of joy. On the one hand, God will gather the dispersed ones, and on the other hand, he will set free those who are confined. God will not totally abandon his people, but will bring the Abrahamic promise of blessing to fulfillment. The expression in the first person "I will" (v. 12) portrays the promise as coming directly from the mouth of the Lord. And the synonymous parallelism with the infinitive absolute construction "I will surely gather (*Qal* or G-stem in Hebrew)" and "I will surely bring together (*Pi'el* or D-stem in Hebrew)," moving from the general Qal to the more intensive Pi'el verbal stem, makes the promise particularly forceful. There is no doubt about it. The images of the sheep in the fold and the flock in the pasture evoke the feeling of peaceful community, security, and abundance. Indeed, in the context of the exploitation of the weak by the powerful, the image of providing protection for weak and docile sheep is very moving. It speaks volumes in language that Micah's rural community can understand. The ordinary people in rural Israel should not lose hope. In fact, God is going to use them to bring restoration to the land.

The terminology of "remnant" is introduced explicitly here for the first time in the prophecy. Although the idea of a faithful remnant is an old one (see Gen 45:7; 2 Sam 14:7; 2 Kgs 19:4, 31; Isa 37:4, 32), it becomes a major theological motif during the Babylonian exile, especially in the prophecies of Ezekiel and Jeremiah. Even though many among the covenant people will fall away, God will always preserve for himself a small remnant who will remain faithful. This remnant will not only remain faithful, but will be the catalyst for future renewal and growth (see Jer 23:3). This idea underscores the biblical principle that God often blesses the many through the few. The term occurs five times in Micah and is a major theological theme that runs throughout the book (Mic 4:7; 5:6–7; 7:18).

Verse 13 brings the oracle of salvation to a climax and foreshadows the message of the latter half of the book. There is a change from the peaceful shepherd imagery to that of the powerful military hero. Firstly, a deliverer is introduced who will lead the remnant of Israel from bondage to freedom. The substantive use of the participle, "the one breaking out" (*happorets*), is unique in the Bible and requires comment. The basic meaning of the verb is "to break out" or "to spread forth." The Lord can break forth in judgment (Exod 19:22, 24; Judg 21:15; 2 Sam 6:8) and will break down the walls of his vineyard (Isa 5:5). However, the term is also used in a positive sense denoting the covenant blessing of increase (Gen 28:14; 30:30, 43; Exod 1:12; Isa 54:3). The promise to Jacob (Gen 28:14) that his descendants will spread forth and multiply all over the earth is significant here since in verse 12 the descendants of Jacob are addressed. Evidently, the prophet is recalling the covenant promises to the patriarchs; God has not abandoned his project to bring blessing to all nations through his people. The deliverer is not just the one who judges Israel, he will also judge the nations in order to restore Israel to freedom. Wolff has stated it well, "He intends to gather those who have been scattered and lead forth into freedom those who have been imprisoned."[12] In addition, several terms are used to remind the reader of the deliverance from Egypt. The verbs "to go up" (*'alah*), "to pass through" (*'abar*), and "to go out" (*yatsa*) are key terms used to

---

12. See, *Micah the Prophet*, trans. by Ralph D. Gehrke (Philadelphia: Fortress, 1981), 59.

describe the exodus from Egypt.[13] Therefore, God's future act of deliverance will be like a new exodus in its power and significance. The last line of the oracle is clearer in the identification of this coming deliverer. He will be their king, a descendant of David, but even more startling, he will be none other than God himself. We interpret the Hebrew copula ("and") epexegetically, i.e. it provides an explanation of the previous expression. We may note that the prophets Haggai and Zechariah regard this prophecy as being (partially) fulfilled in their time with the return and the rebuilding of the temple (Hag 1:12–14; 2:2; Zech 8:6, 11–12). But, of course, the greater fulfillment happens with the coming of the Lord Jesus Christ in the New Testament.

Many scholars regard these verses as exilic or post-exilic and apply them to Jerusalem's deliverance from Sennacherib in 701 BC (2 Kgs 19:31). However, we find this interpretation not very convincing. Firstly, there is no evidence that these verses are exilic or post-exilic. As mentioned in the introduction, the book of Micah already existed by the end of the seventh century BC, some time before the exile. The concepts of "remnant" (Gen 45:7; Deut 3:11; 2 Sam 14:7; Isa 10:20–22; Amos 5:15) and the people of God as "flock" (Gen 48:15; 49:24; Num 27:12; 2 Sam 5:2; 7:7; Amos 3:12) have already taken root in the traditions of Israel before the Babylonian exile. There is nothing in the text that prohibits a pre-exilic provenance. Secondly, the events of the siege and deliverance of Jerusalem in 701 BC do not accord with the description of the salvation oracle here. As far as we know, a "remnant" was not gathered and there was no "breaking out": for whatever reason the Assyrians simply left. If this prophecy was written after the event, surely the writer would have done a better job.

Christians who live in a non-Christian environment and who often strain under the ungodly behavior of church leaders, wandering around without a spiritual home or being confined within oppressive sectarian structures, may take heart from the hope that Micah's message provides. God is keenly aware and very much concerned about their disappointment, disillusionment, and strain. Many congregations have been decimated by pastors who cause havoc and split churches; often only a remnant survives. Christians are scattered and have no spiritual home, or they are confined and imprisoned by the structures of their authoritarian church. Indeed, the evil one wants to scatter and confine. But, in spite of such discouraging sets of circumstances, God can change the

---

13. For example, see Exod 3:8, 10–12, 17; 12:12, 17, 23, 31, 38; 13:3–4, 14–16, 18–19; 15:15; 17:5; 20:2; Deut 1:21–22, 27; 4:22, 28, 37, 45–46.

situation. God plans to gather his sheep, set them free, and unite them together in communities with ample pasture and full of joy. The text portrays a beautiful sequence from gathering lost sheep into a flock to find pasture and joy.

This new movement of renewal will be characterized by the divine action of gathering, it will be effected without human manipulation, it will be a truly spiritual movement. Interestingly, the prophecy does not mention material blessing of land or prosperity. Rather, the main characteristic, it appears, will be the focus on the actions of the deliverer or the king as their head. This is what Jesus does in the gospel and in the world today. According to the Gospel of John, Jesus said:

> I am the good shepherd; I know my sheep and my sheep know me – just as the Father knows me and I know the Father – and I lay down my life for the sheep. I have other sheep that are not of this sheep pen. I must bring them also. They too will listen to my voice, and there shall be one flock and one shepherd. (John 10:14–16)

We may expect that scattered and confined Christians will again experience a strong divine urge to draw close to God in true worship. They will have new discoveries of the grace and knowledge of the Lord Jesus that will enable them to break through all kinds of barriers to unite in Christian fellowship where they will find nutritious pasture and deep joy. Wherever this happens, we know that there the prophecy of Micah is being fulfilled.

THE REMNANT

The concept of "remnant," which is referred to five times in the book of Micah (Mic 2:12; 4:7; 4:7–8; 7:18), is an important theme in biblical theology. It is also closely related, like all significant themes, to salvation history and covenant theology. The main Hebrew terms used to articulate the concept is the feminine noun *she'erit*, its masculine counterpart *she'ar*, and the masculine noun *yether*. The first two nouns basically refer to "what is left over," and is translated with terms such as "remainder," "residue," "remnant," and the "rest," and may refer to either animate or inanimate things. The latter term also means "remainder" or "remnant," but in certain contexts it has the related idea of excess, which extends to the notions of "abundance," "excellence," and "superiority." It should be pointed out that other terms are also used to refer to the theological concept of remnant, and that the use of the afore-mentioned terms is not always theologically significant.

The concept of "remnant" basically refers to a small or select group of people who has gone through some form of suffering and are singled out for a special divine purpose, which can either involve judgment (2 Kgs 21:14; Isa 14:22; Zeph 1:4) or salvation (2 Kgs 19:30–31; Jer 23:3; Zech 8:11–12). Although biblical authors use the idea of the "remnant" differently, one may trace a steady development of the theme through the canonical record from the Pentateuch into the Former and Latter Prophets. Some scholars have distinguished three aspects or three stages in the development of the concept, consisting of the historical remnant, the faithful remnant, and finally the eschatological remnant.[1]

The remnant, which becomes a major theme in the Writing Prophets, can be traced back to the early chapters of Genesis. After the fall into sin (Gen 3), humanity develops according to two lines, one through Cain and the other through Seth, which is an outworking of the *protoevangelium* (i.e "the first gospel") in Genesis 3:15. Rebellion and evil continue to increase throughout the world as history develops through the line of Cain, but God is faithful in preserving a group of people – a remnant – who retains faith and through whom God preserves a godly seed. Seth, Enosh, Enoch, Noah, and Shem stand in this line. As humanity becomes progressively more defiant, God's redemptive action narrows in to focus on Abraham and his family, who are chosen to be the channel of God's blessing for the whole world. The idea of the remnant becomes explicitly evident in the Joseph story, in which he undergoes rejection and suffering for the greater purpose of preserving a remnant (Gen 45:7). Later in the exodus from slavery and the desert wanderings, even though most Israelites are rebellious and long to go back to Egypt, a select group of people remained faithful – Moses, Aaron, Miriam, Caleb, and Joshua – and because of them God is able to bring his people into the

Promised Land. Except for Deborah and Gideon, the accounts in the book of Judges are basically a continuous narrative about depravity and lawlessness. It is only with Hannah and Samuel that a new remnant appears through whom God speaks again to his people, calling them back to covenant faithfulness. With the establishment of the monarchy, David and his royal family become the remnant through whom God's covenant is preserved and carried forward, but only until the split of the kingdom in 929 BC. With apostasy in Israel, there is a shift from the judges and kings as the guardians of the covenant to the prophetic community. Elijah, Elisha, and the 7000 faithful who did not bow to Baal become the faithful remnant. Elijah and Elisha's miracles and intimate relationship with God demonstrate that God now works through his prophets to guide and protect his people. The remnant becomes more clearly defined as the purified prophetic community, those who trust in the Lord. Around the time of the Assyrian and Babylonian exile there is a subtle change away from a group belonging to national Israel to faithfulness to the Lord as the new determining factor for being the remnant.

In the book of Isaiah, the transition from the historical remnant to the faithful remnant, and finally to the eschatological remnant is most clearly perceived. Despite the devastation of Zion through corruption and war, God's people are going to be restored (Isa 2:3; 62:6–12). The remnant plays a key role in the transformation of Zion, which in turn will bring salvation history to fulfillment with the ingathering of the Gentiles into God's restored city (Isa 10:19–22; 11:11, 16; 28:5; 37:31). After the devastating effects of the Babylonian exile, the Jews found themselves without a king, a land, and a hope (Isa 40:27–28). However, within this group of exiles, a remnant refused to give up hope, but continued to trust that the Lord could and would change their situation. Indeed, they discovered the Lord's plan was that after refinement through suffering they would become the catalyst for a new exodus that would lead to the restoration of Zion (Isa 40:9; 41:8–16; 46:3–4; 48:9–11; 52:11). The message of the suffering servant provides the kernel of this new theology (Isa 42:1–7; 49:1–7; 50:4–9; 53:1–12). The final chapters of Isaiah look beyond the borders of Israel to the eschatological future where people from all nations will come and join the remnant (Isa 17:3; 42:4; 49:8–12, 23; 51:5; 56:3–8), culminating with the creation of a new heavens and earth (Isa 65:17–25; 66:22–23). The chief identity maker of this new community will be trust in the Lord, rather than ethnic heritage (Isa 8:17; 26:8; 30:15–18; 40:31; 66:2). In addition, this new community will continue the role of the suffering servant in being a witness to the whole world (Isa 42:6–7; 43:10; 49:1–3, 23; 60:1–3; 62:1–2; 66:18–19).

In the book of Micah, God will first gather the remnant (Mic 2:12), then the remnant will become a strong nation (Mic 4:7), and finally the remnant will become a blessing to the nations (Mic 5:7–8); all because God will forgive the sins of his remnant (Mic 7:18). God will use the remnant as an instrument to advance salvation history, fulfilling the promises of the Abrahamic covenant. In the later prophets, because of the important role of the remnant in salvation history, there is a big concern for the survival of the remnant (Jer 24:8; 40:15; 42:2; 44:7; Ezek 9:8). Indeed, the existence of a faithful remnant, however small, is seen as a sign of God's favor (Ezra 9:8–15).

Although the term "remnant" does not often occur in the New Testament, the crucial role that the believing community – the disciples of Jesus – plays in fulfilling the purposes of God is unmistakable. All the themes related to salvation history in the Old Testament find their resolution in the New Testament. Jesus is the suffering servant who fulfills Old Testament prophecy[2] and the one who gathers God's people into the new Zion, i.e. the church.[3] The disciples, by continuing to fulfill the role of the servant, become the agents through whom God brings salvation to the world (Matt 28:18–20; Acts 1:8; 2:41–47). The church is called to engage in missionary activity. Consequently, when James deliberated on the inclusion of the Gentiles into the people of God, he quoted the words from Amos 9:11–12, "After this I will return, and I will rebuild the tent of David that has fallen; I will rebuild its ruins, and I will restore it, that the remnant of mankind may seek the Lord, and all the Gentiles who are called by my name, says the Lord, who makes these things known from of old" (Acts 15:16–18 ESV). In other words, the ingathering of the Gentiles into the church is the fulfillment of Old Testament prophecy about the future remnant that God will gather. So too, Paul quoted the words of Isaiah 10:22–23 and Isaiah 1:9 about the remnant of Israel and applied them to Jews who believe in Jesus (Rom 9:27–29; see also Rom 11:1–5). In line with the message of the Old Testament prophets, the main identity marker of this new community is not racial identity, but faith in Jesus (Rom 10:9–15; Gal 3:6–9, 28–29).

---

1. Gerhard F. Hasel, "Remnant," in *International Standard Bible Encyclopedia* (ed. Geoffrey W. Bromley; 4 vols.; Completely revised and reset ed.; Grand Rapids, MI: Eerdmans, 1988), 4: 130. Also see, Gerhard F. Hasel, *The Remnant: The History and Theology of the Remnant*.
2. For example, see Matt 8:17; Mark 12:18–21; Luke 53:12; John 12:38; Acts 8:32; 13:34; 1 Pet 2:24.
3. See Matt 13:30; 23:37; 24:31; John 10:16; 11:52; see also Eph 1:22; 2:11–14; Heb 12:22; Rev 14:1.

MICAH 3

Chapter 3 continues to pronounce judgment upon God's people. But whereas in chapter 2 the rich landowners who exploit ordinary people were castigated, now the civil and spiritual leaders are singled out for judgment. Micah's warning becomes more pointed and provocative as he develops his message of judgment and destruction.

3:1–4 Judgment upon Leaders because of Injustice

The opening statement, "Then I said," ties the oracle of chapter 3 with chapter 2; there is a further development in the prophet's message of condemnation.[14] The keyword "rulers" (literally, "heads") makes this development explicit. There is a big contrast with the description of the Lord's leadership as a shepherd at the "head" of his people in the last part of chapter 2 and the "heads" who devour the people of Jacob in the opening statement of the next oracle. According to Smith, "These 'heads' and 'leaders' were not kings or priests but officials who functioned as judges in the city gates."[15] The second command "listen" or "hear" in the prophecy stands at the beginning of the section and implies that the rulers of God's people are not obeying the word of the Lord. Even though the terms "Jacob" and "Israel" are used, it appears that the southern kingdom is addressed in this section (see Mic 3:12). We assume that judgment has already fallen upon Samaria, but there is still hope for Jerusalem. The parallelism, the change from "Jacob" to "Israel," may also imply that the Judean rulers have become corrupt like the rulers of the northern kingdom.

The rhetorical question, "Should you not embrace justice?" points out that the nation's rulers abandoned fair processes, righteousness, and mercy. The term "justice" has a broad semantic range, including "judgment," "decision," "proper procedure," "justice," "right," "rectitude," "ordinance," "custom," "legal decision," "legal case," etc. It essentially summarizes the basic function of a leader or judge. The prophet's insistence on the need for justice can be understood in light of the Old Testament covenant context, because it lies at the center of God's purpose for Israel and the world. God chose Abraham in order that his descendants might establish a society of justice and righteousness, and so become a light for the nations (see Gen 12:1–3; 18:17–19). Therefore,

---

14. According to H. W. Wolff, "The written formulation goes back to Micah himself," in *Micah the Prophet*, trans. by Ralph D. Gehrke (Philadelphia: Fortress, 1981), 65. It seems that Micah has some knowledge of what is happening in Jerusalem. He is not addressing the king, but officials and judges, but they are not mentioned by name.
15. Smith, *Micah-Malachi*, 31.

Micah 1–3: The Message of Destruction

there is a big emphasis in the Mosaic law on the need for judges and rulers to be paragons of justice (Exod 23:1–9; Deut 16:18-20; 17:14-20; 27:11-26). Consequently, the Deuteronomistic history castigates those who disregard justice (1 Sam 8:1-3; 1 Sam 24:17; 2 Sam 4:11) and celebrates those who maintain justice (2 Sam 8:15; 1 Kgs 3:10-12, 28; 10:9).

Whereas the problem in chapter 1 is identified as idolatry, in chapters 2 and 3 the problem becomes one of exploitation and injustice. The prophet's logic infers that idolatry leads to injustice. Therefore, the real issue of concern in Micah is the same as the earlier prophets of Hosea and Amos (see Hos 4:1–3; 10:12; 12:6; Amos 2:6–7; 4:1; 5:15, 24; 6:12; 8:4–6). In fact, the link between idolatry and cruelty is also a major lesson in the book of Jonah, which provides the immediate canonical context to the book of Micah. Jonah 2:8, which occurs right at the center of the book, provides the main theme and should be translated as, "Those who worship vain idols, abandon mercy."[16] Jonah has constructed his own idol of a prejudiced nationalistic ideology which made him indifferent to the plight of others. But whereas the indifference in the book of Jonah was directed towards outsiders or Gentiles, in the book of Micah it is directed towards insiders or the people of God. The leaders did not heed the message of Hosea and Amos, now through Micah they have another chance to hear and repent. God is amazingly patient with his people.

Verses 2 and 3 describe the characteristics of the evil rulers and judges. The words are reminiscent of Amos's injunction to hate what is evil and love what is good (Amos 5:15). Despite the stark warnings of many prophets, the rulers still did not amend their ways. Their attitudes regarding good and evil are displayed in their behavior of exploiting ordinary people. Micah's language, which extends the image of the people as sheep from chapter 2:12, is very graphic and is intended to illustrate the heinous nature of the rulers' action and the pain it brought to God's people. They had no regard for justice, nor for the suffering of the poor; their hearts had become cold like ice. In fact, they had become cannibals! Of course, one should not interpret the passage literally or assign a meaning to every particular word, rather as poetry the language is symbolic and the details contribute to the overall picture of shock and cruelty.

Verse 4 describes God's judgment upon callous and unjust leadership; God will cease to answer their prayers. Similarly, in Proverbs we read, "Whoever shuts their ears to the cry of the poor will also cry out and not be answered"

---

16. See J. Ferreira, "A Note on Jonah 2.8: Idolatry and Inhumanity in Israel," *The Bible Translator* 63 (2012), 28–38.

(Prov 21:13). Since civil rulers are addressed here, the content or request of their prayers probably relates to natural disasters, epidemics, social stability, economic growth, and national security, the main concerns of civil leaders. These concerns or risks are recurrent issues for any nation or society, and many are averted through earnest prayer (compare 1 Kgs 8:30–53; 2 Chr 7:12–14). In the future, however, these crises will threaten and will overtake the people. Judgment will not come immediately, but will come sporadically over time until the leadership and nation collapse. God's intention through recurrent disasters is to awaken the ungodly and to lead them to repentance. God will not save them when they face threats and challenges, even if they pray, unless they sincerely repent with changed behavior. But it appears "the rice has already been cooked" (大米已经成饭了 *da mi yi jing cheng fan le*), their evil cannot be undone.

The account of the rulers in 2 Kings 15 provides an illustration of the historical context for Micah's vivid language. Israelite rulers were indiscriminately devouring one another and ordinary people for their own selfish ends. Since King Azariah of Judah turned a blind eye to idolatry, God afflicted him with leprosy, and although he probably prayed for healing he did not repent and was not healed (2 Kgs 15:4–5). In the northern kingdom, Shallum murdered King Zechariah in public and then assumed leadership (2 Kgs 15:10), only to be replaced one month later by Menahem who massacred an entire village because it did not support his conspiracy, even ripping open the pregnant women (2 Kgs 15:13–16). Menahem was very corrupt and pillaged both the rich and the poor to shore up his reign (2 Kgs 15:19–20). Menahem's son and successor, Pekahiah, was in turn murdered by Pekah (2 Kgs 15:24–25). Over a period of twenty years Israel had no less than eight kings. It was a period of great instability, corruption, and exploitation of the poor. The narrative in 2 Kings 15 concludes by stating that, "In those days the LORD began to send Rezin king of Aram and Pekah son of Remaliah against Judah" (2 Kgs 15:37). It was not enough for the Israelite kings to exploit and murder their own brothers and sisters, they also conspired with Gentiles to turn against their southern cousins. With this background it is easy to understand the deep emotional anguish of Micah's strong denunciation of the rulers.

WORLDLINESS AMONG CHRISTIAN LEADERS

Corrupt officials are often observed in the world. Rulers exploiting innocent civilians are all too common in Asia. In China there is a saying among the common people that corrupt officials "breed like flies and emerge in endless streams." For an atheistic country, it is perhaps not a surprise to observe such widespread corruption, and we as Christians often like to point the finger and shake our heads. However, it is important to note that Micah is not denouncing injustice in the world, he is exposing and condemning corruption within the covenant community.

The central issue of this chapter is about leadership, or rather the lack of just, virtuous, and honorable leadership among God's people. It is a commonly known truth that the health of any nation or organization is determined by its leadership. Leaders shape the values, culture, and behavior of those under them, and so it is not surprising that the moral character of a group of people will never rise above its leadership. This general truth also applies to the church. When the leadership was godly in the Old Testament, society was upright and just, but when the leadership was ungodly, "everyone did as they saw fit" (Judg 21:25). We see the same scenario in church history and in churches today. When the church's leadership is ignorant, self-centered, and hypocritical, there is much disarray, partiality, and indolence among ordinary believers. Church history is awash with such examples from the Middle Ages until today, whether it is the church in the West or in the East, corrupt clergy breeds superstition and barbarity among ordinary people. It is shocking, and a perpetual shame for the Christian church, to recall the behavior of Christian leaders, who for the sake of their own selfish gratification obtained power through bribery, maintained mistresses, enriched themselves and their families, and tortured and killed their rivals.

At the time of Micah's prophecy, the leaders of Judah were unjust, habitually abusing their power for personal and selfish gain. They did not serve first and foremost for the well-being of the people, but pursued their own personal agendas. Most leaders not only failed to live according to the moral requirements of God's law, they also neglected biblical principles in the execution of their communal duties. No doubt, they could cite many reasons to justify their behavior, but, from God's perspective – the only perspective that ultimately matters – most leaders were failures, unjust, and dishonest. According to Micah's message, these leaders stand condemned before God. Likewise, when Paul outlines the requirements for elders and deacons he places most emphasis on matters of character, rather than worldly success or talent. The leader must "be above reproach, faithful to his wife, temperate, self-controlled, respectable, hospitable, able to teach, not given to drunkenness, not violent but gentle, not quarrelsome, not a lover of money" (1 Tim 3:1–13; see also Titus 1:5–9).

> Furthermore, Paul often warns Christians not to be gullible by blindly following worldly leaders in the church (Rom 16:17–20; 1 Cor 1:10–13; 3:18-21; 11:1–5; 1 Tim 1:18–20; 2 Tim 4:10).
>
> Micah's prophecy is an urgent wake-up call to all who serve in leadership positions in the church and in Christian organizations – whether they are bishops, managers, principals, directors, superintendents, pastors, elders, deacons, teachers, or administrators. Christians tend to believe the best about the church's leaders and hold them in high regard. However, we know that Christian leaders, however holy or dedicated they may be, are still sinful human beings and are prone to all forms of temptation. Leaders not only need constantly to examine their own hearts and behavior; they also need to be accountable to others. In the Old Testament, even the king was to examine his actions daily according to God's law (Deut 17:18–20; see also Josh 1:7–8) and was held accountable by the prophets (see 1 Sam 15:22–23; 2 Sam 12:1–15). In the New Testament, even Paul, the chief apostle, considered himself to be accountable to others and was very transparent in his ministry (Rom 1:11–13; 15:22–31; 1 Cor 4:1–5; 2 Cor 1:12–24; 1 Thess 2:1–12; see also Acts 14:27). Christian leaders must not be motivated by selfish ambitions, status, or financial gain. They must not abuse their power, but listen to advice, be open to scrutiny, and work under accountability structures to avoid temptation and to be beyond suspicion. For those involved in Christian service, these are major issues which require constant and serious attention.

3:5–7 Judgment upon Prophets because of Deception

In this oracle Micah begins to denounce the prophets. There was not just a problem with the rich and the civil rulers of Israel, even the prophets – who were supposed to be the last bastion of truth – have departed from the Lord and have become corrupt. They too, like the rest, are just seeking their own profit and are in cahoots with the other evil-doers. Instead of protesting, they are accomplices in the crimes of social injustice that are being committed with impunity. In fact, the main responsibility for the sin of God's people is laid at the feet of the prophets. They are making God's people wander in circles like the Israelites wandered in the desert, not able to enter the Promised Land. Isaiah had already identified this problem; the leaders misled God's people and the prophets taught lies (Isa 3:12; 9:14–16). The expression "if they have something to eat" (literally, "who when they are biting with their teeth") is conditional and refers to banqueting. According to Wolff, "What comes out of their mouth depends on what has first gone into it."[17] Basically, these prophets preach according to their remuneration. If they are well rewarded they preach messages of peace, but when they are not well paid they bring messages of doom. The expression "they prepare to wage war" literally means "they consecrate a war" (i.e. they use "spiritual" language) and means to oppose those who do not benefit them.[18] They are engrossed with their own personal and political agendas; God's concerns are far away from their hearts.

We may again cite another letter from Lachish that illustrates the message that these false prophets were delivering to the people of Judah just before the Babylonian exile. In the letter, an officer by the name of Hoshayahu (meaning "Yahweh is my Salvation"), akin to the name of the biblical prophet Hosea, wrote to his commander, Ya'osh, at Lachish. The letter reads:

> To my lord Ya'osh. May Yahweh cause my lord to hear the news of peace, even now, even now. Who is your servant, but a dog that my lord should remember his servant?[19]

We may well surmise that the optimism of the officer about "peace" was fueled by the message of the false prophets like those whom Micah was describing in his prophecy. Many Judean towns were lost already and Jerusalem was about to fall into the hands of the Babylonians, and yet, astoundingly, the people were still expecting peace from the Lord. We also note in the letter that the officer received some benefit from his master, suggesting that the prayer for peace could have been precipitated by the benefit received, which again illustrates the situation that Micah was addressing. Pronouncement of peace and blessing could be procured with financial and social rewards.

Verses 6 and 7 announce God's judgment upon these false prophets. God will no longer reveal himself to them and will be silent when they cry out to him. The judgment reminds us of the story of Eli and his sons, who forfeited the word of God through their lethargy and decadence. Since they have no message from the Lord, they will just make things up as they go along, pulling entertaining messages out of thin air. However, inevitably, sooner or later their ignorance and confusion will become evident to all (see Isa 28:7). God will frustrate their preaching (see Isa 44:25) and in the end their voices will be

---

17. Wolff, *Micah the Prophet*, 71.
18. See C. F. Keil and F. Delitsch, *Commentary on the Old Testament Volume 10: Minor Prophets*, trans. by James Martin (Grand Rapids, MI: Eerdmans, 1973), 452.
19. James B. Pritchard, *The Ancient Near East, Volume I, An Anthology of Texts and Pictures* (Princeton, NJ: Princeton University Press, 1973), 212.

silenced; they will lose all respect and will be ridiculed in society. The word that Micah uses for "divination" normally occurs in the context of wizardry and soothsaying, practices which were forbidden for God's people (Lev 19:26, 31; Deut 18:10–14). It may also have a positive connotation relating to decision or insight. However, the term is used here to show that these false preachers of prosperity have no word or insight from God, and are no different from pagan diviners.

DECEITFUL PREACHERS

In this section, prophets or preachers have become the center of Micah's attention. There is an escalating crisis among the people of God: the rich have exploited the poor, then the leaders and administrators have become corrupt, but now even the prophets are hypocrites. Noticeably, the institutions and the leaders of the covenant community have abandoned God's standards and are pursuing their own agendas. Even the preachers of God's people are driven by greed for money, power, and prestige. Unfortunately, Micah does not just describe the situation in ancient Israel, his words are also an apt portrayal of many churches and Christian leaders today.

Financial corruption is rife in many sections of the Asian church. For example, David W. Virtue reports that, according to intelligence authorities, 15 out of 21 Anglican bishops of the Church of South India, which is the biggest Protestant denomination in India, have been tainted with corruption.[1] He writes that, "Corruption has emanated from the highest levels of the church – its bishops – with charges of tax fraud, cronyism, nepotism, money hijacked from land deals, hospital fraud, stolen Tsunami funds, vote buying, and much more." It is reported that the General Secretary of the Church diverted two million dollars intended for the 2004 Tsunami victims to his family enterprises.

Many in the Christian world were also shocked in 2014 when South Korean pastor David Yonggi Cho, who is the founder of the world's largest mega-church, Yoido Full Gospel Church, was convicted of embezzling 12 million US dollars.[2] The church is still under investigation for misappropriating US$500 million. The story also revealed that the leadership and Pastor Cho were frequently counseled by concerned elders to be more transparent and to improve the management of the church's finances, but they ignored the advice. South Korean Christians are increasingly disillusioned with organized religion and thousands are leaving the church every year. Shallow teaching, emotional extremes, greed, blind compliance, and hypocrisy among church leaders have led to thousands of "unchurched Christians" who have left the organized church. God will hold the leadership of the church accountable for this state of affairs.

Micah 1–3: The Message of Destruction

Financial corruption does not only occur in mega-churches with multi-million dollar budgets, it also occurs in small churches. In northern China, there was a pastor of a Chinese family church who was not willing to have the church's accounts scrutinized by others. Some members suspected that there was financial mismanagement, but when they raised the issue with the leadership they were severely attacked by the pastor, who accused them of heresy and promptly excommunicated them from the church.

When there is financial misconduct, like City Harvest Church in Singapore and Yoido Full Gospel Church in Korea, there is often also a problem with the church's theology. For example, many preachers who have been implicated in financial mismanagement and corruption, whether in Asia or the West, are proponents of the so-called "prosperity gospel." The theology of the "prosperity gospel" closely links Christian faith with success at work, in business, and in society. There is also an emphasis on miracles, healing, emotional highs, and having fun. The leaders of such churches are often paraded as model Christians, being good-looking, trendy, healthy, affluent, and popular. They justify their approach on the basis of establishing "seeker sensitive" and "culturally relevant" churches. However, from a biblical perspective this increasingly popular version of the Christian message is problematic. The Bible does not promise perfect health and worldly success for those who would follow Jesus, instead it talks about tribulation, cross-bearing, and persecution. Clearly, human aspirations and the desires of the world are often at odds with the values of God's kingdom. The Bible encourages Christians to pursue humility, self-denial, simplicity, poverty, honesty, purity, patience, justice, mercy, and faith. Proponents of the "prosperity gospel" do not preach about sin and repentance, they do not focus on the cross, and they do not nourish the Lord's sheep with real spiritual food, but twist the message of the Bible. Their teaching focuses on achieving one's goals, reaching one's full potential, and being healthy and happy. This message, of course, is very popular and easily attracts thousands of adherents, but the more important question is whether or not we are faithful to the biblical message that exposes human depravity and that calls us to repentance and faith.

Micah's message calls for preachers and teachers in Asia to examine themselves. Are we following the latest fashions of the world, often coming from America, or are we focusing on the message of the cross, even though some may find it simplistic and others may be offended? There is a choice to be made: to be popular with the world or to be truthful to God. Preachers and teachers need to take note. Micah's message announces that God is not inattentive, but is very much aware of the motivation and message of preachers. God will honor those who preach the gospel accurately with pure motivation, but will forsake those who follow their own agendas. James Limburg observes:

> Micah's diagnosis warns that it is still possible for a theologian to become more concerned about fees than faith, about honoraria than honor. The response of God may then be the same: silence. The theologian experiences a burn-out or flame-out, with no more fire, no more steam, no more passion for justice or for God. Then the theologian has broken with his or her vocation. There is no contact with *theos*, and thus no longer an authentic *logos*, and the preacher is left with nothing to preach.[3]
>
> The radio may be on, but if no signal comes from the transmitter, no message will be received. There will only be hissing and noise. Listeners will sooner or later turn the radio off. So too, the babble of false theology, however beautifully it may be packaged, will turn out to be just hissing and noise. Listeners will become disillusioned and turn away, and the broadcasters will soon be without an audience and be left out in the cold. God will expose these preachers to the world as frauds.
>
> These serious themes about justice, integrity, and truthfulness in the Old Testament are just as prominent in the New Testament. Jesus often warns us against the hypocrisy of the Pharisees (e.g. Matt 5–7; 23) and Paul frequently alerts us about false teachers in the church (e.g. Phil 1:15–17; 3:2–6, 18–19; 1 Thess 4:6; 1 Tim 1:37; 4:1–5; 2 Tim 3:1–8; 4:3–5). Therefore, it is surprising how little attention preachers and teachers give to these warnings today. Church history and the examples we cited of corruption in the church demonstrate clearly that wrong motives and selfish interests are very prevalent among church leaders. Yet, it seldom occurs to us that we may be the people that the text describes. We are ignoring these biblical warnings at our own peril.
>
> ---
>
> 1. See www.virtueonline.org (accessed on March 27, 2013).
> 2. Because of his age, Yonggi Cho received a suspended sentence.
> 3. James Limburg, *Hosea-Micah. Interpretation: A Bible Commentary for Teaching and Preaching* (Atlanta, GA: John Knox Press, 1988), 177.

3:8 The Response of the Prophet

In verse 8 Micah compares himself with the false prophets. In the Hebrew text there is an adversative copula ("but") which indicates a strong contrast with the preceding verses. The NASB translated it as "on the other hand." The character of Micah's person and the nature of Micah's ministry are very different from those of the prosperity preachers. Micah is the true prophet of God's people; indeed, God never leaves himself without a witness. In contrast with the false prophets, Micah is filled with power, which is defined in terms of the Spirit

Micah 1–3: The Message of Destruction

of the Lord, justice, and might. He has the power to operate in the sphere of the Spirit and to carry out justice. Micah's experience, life, and perspective are very different from the other prophets. His identity is not defined by a title, or a position, or a reward, but by the Spirit of the Lord, and by a courageous and righteous life. Micah's bravery in confronting the *status quo* reminds us of the courage of the prophet Nathan when he confronted David over his exploitation of Uriah and Beersheba (2 Sam 12:1–15) and about the prophet Oded when he confronted the Israelite army over its exploitation of Judah (2 Chr 28:8–15). Because Micah was filled with the Spirit of the Lord and lived a righteous life, he was able to preach with conviction and clarity. He did not shy away from "calling a spade a spade;" instead, he unambiguously exposed Israel's failure and shortcomings. Micah's experience foreshadows the greater prophet who is to come: Jesus of Nazareth (see Deut 18:15–19; Isa 11:2; 61:1). It is significant to note that the power of the Spirit often comes to the fore in the Bible in the context of conflict and opposition (Matt 10:19–20; John 14:16–18; 16:21; Judges 3:10; 11:29; 14:6,19; Isa 11:2; 42:1; 61:1–2). When things are going well and there is no danger, it is easy to stand up for the truth and righteousness. However, it is a different story to speak up under adversity and the threat of persecution.

Micah's confidence and determination may serve to encourage preachers who strive to remain faithful to the Lord amidst much opposition and temptation. Preachers must know both the calling of the Lord and also the power of the Lord to carry out their ministries, which come through the operation of the Spirit. On the one hand, preachers must be engrossed with the knowledge of God's word, but also, on the other hand, they need spiritual insight and power to teach and apply God's word within their specific contexts. Whereas the first aspect relates to personal discipline and the dedication to study God's word, the second aspect relates to prayer and the obtaining of God's power to act with justice, integrity, and courage. It is important to note – in view of common misunderstanding – that the "Spirit of the LORD" refers to more than an emotional experience, it refers to the capacity to understand God's word accurately, to live it out sacrificially, and to proclaim it effectively to others (see 1 Cor 2:1–5; 10–11; 4:17–21; 2 Cor 3:4–18; 4:1–17). Thus, Paul exhorts Timothy, "Preach the word; be prepared in season and out of season; correct, rebuke and encourage – with great patience and careful instruction" (2 Tim 4:2). Furthermore, as mentioned before, the word "justice" may also mean proper "discernment" or refer to a right "decision," for example, Micah is able to distinguish between right and wrong, make a sound judgment, and then he is courageous enough to declare it. He does not sit on the fence, but is prepared to tell the truth.

Asian pastors are often very reluctant to rock the boat or let others "lose face." In light of the many moral issues that face Christians today, pastors need to discern the will of God from the Scriptures and be more direct and courageous to declare it. The biggest need for the church and the world is still to have preachers, who understand God's word, are filled with the Spirit, able to discern right from wrong, act with justice and integrity, and then unflinchingly to proclaim God's word without fear or prejudice.

3:9–12 Summary

Verses 9 to 12 provide a summary and a conclusion to the Message of Destruction, the first section of the book of Micah. The command "hear this" recalls the previous injunction to the leadership of the people to take note in verse 1. By addressing the leaders of the people with the traditional terminology, "Jacob" and "Israel," Micah is again reminding them of their history and covenantal responsibilities. "Jacob" means "supplanter" or "cheat," but through God's grace "Jacob" became "Israel," which means "struggling" and "prevailing" with God. The people of God can learn from their history, rely on God's mercy, and change; "Jacob" may yet become "Israel," and obtain God's protection and blessing. However, unfortunately, the leaders continue to practice injustice and have no regard for what is right. Judah has become like Israel, and Jerusalem like Samaria. There is no difference between the three major institutions of society – the rulers, the priests,[20] and the prophets. They are all the same, aiding one another for social and financial advancement. They have no regard for God's truth and for the well-being of the common people. Even the prophets, who were supposed to be the guardians of truth and godliness, have become preachers of prosperity for payment. Yet, to make matters worse, despite their corruption and deceit, they still pretend to be very spiritual – they have not rejected religion – and claim that God is with them and that there will be no disaster. However, Micah, with the power of the Spirit, exposes their folly and true motives. With the rich landowners in chapter 2, we now have a gang of four who are responsible for the demise of the people of God.

---

20. This is the only place in the book of Micah where the priests are mentioned. Priests are mentioned only once probably because Micah in Moresheth lived far away from the temple and did not have much to do with the priests in Jerusalem.

Micah 1–3: The Message of Destruction

Whereas verses 9 to 11 diagnosed the problem, verse 12 provides the prognosis. The result of their actions is inescapable: there will be disaster and destruction. Prophecies of doom first spoken against Samaria during the time of Jotham are now addressed to Jerusalem in the time of Hezekiah. As mentioned in our introduction, Micah 3:12 is quoted in Jeremiah 26:18 and demonstrates Micah's prophecies were written down before the fall of Jerusalem. But also, it is informative to note that Jeremiah regards Hezekiah and the people of his time, that is the period after the fall of Samaria, as the recipients of Micah's prophecies (Jer 26:16–19). The prophecies about Samaria, a city which appeared much more impenetrable than Jerusalem, have already been fulfilled. Even today, the distinction of Samara is that it is one of the biggest archaeological sites – an ancient ruin – in the territory of the West Bank (see Figure 9). Disaster will also come upon Zion; unless the leadership repent and change, Jerusalem like Samaria will become a ruin. The word "rubble" or "ruin" in Micah 3:12 links the conclusion of the first section with the prophecy about Samaria becoming "rubble" or a "ruin" in Micah 1:6. The same word is used (*'i*), but whereas it is singular in Micah 1:6, the plural ("ruins") is used in Micah 3:16. It appears that the destruction of Jerusalem will be even more devastating than that which fell upon Samaria. Most likely, then, the prophecy about the fall of Samaria has already been fulfilled, and, therefore, served as a stark warning for the southern kingdom. The big lesson of Samaria's destruction is that covenant privileges do not make one immune to God's judgment; it is actions that count, as Paul reminded his readers in his letter to the church in Rome, "For it is not those who hear the law who are righteous in God's sight, but it is those who obey the law who will be declared righteous" (Rom 2:13).

Figure 9. Ancient ruins of Samaria

However, the gloomy prognosis is not set in stone. Old Testament prophecies were often conditional upon people's response and did not pronounce fatalistic destinies, but left open the possibility of deliverance (see Jer 26:1–4). In this regard, biblical prophecy was quite different from the fatalistic pronouncements of oracles among pagan nations. The early readers of Micah would have been familiar with the story of the Ninevites who despite the message of doom by the prophet Jonah, averted judgment when they repented (Jonah 3). Therefore, this dark prophecy of destruction upon Jerusalem was intended to warn and to rouse the leaders of God's people to repentance. If the leaders do not repent and amend their ways, the same judgment will come upon them, but if they repent they may anticipate a more optimistic future. Similarly, the image of "ploughing" taken from Micah's rural environment invites reflection. On the one hand, there is destruction as the soil is being broken up, but, on the other hand, ploughing also prepares for a new sowing and a fresh harvest. Out of apparent defeat and destruction, there could be a new beginning. Judgment may yet lead to salvation. Hence, Micah's prophecy of destruction still contains hope. Indeed, when we turn to where Micah is quoted in Jeremiah, we note that the early readers of Micah did not interpret the prophecy of judgment as being inevitable. The elders of the land pointed out that Hezekiah did not kill Micah for speaking against Jerusalem, but instead repented. "Did Hezekiah king of Judah or anyone else in Judah put him to death? Did not Hezekiah fear the LORD and seek his favor? And did not the LORD relent, so that he did not bring the disaster he pronounced against them?" (Jer 26:19).

Finally, in the last line, the expression "the temple hill" (literally, "the mountain of the house") refers to the temple in Jerusalem. Perhaps, the author is avoiding the term "temple," because in his mind it had already ceased to be the holy place where the Lord resides. Due to the corruption and defiled worship of the priests it is no longer the holy place or the temple of the Lord. This judgment on the temple also recalls the opening words of the book of Micah, which insinuates that God's real temple is in heaven, and that he is coming down to judge all the high places of the earth, including the temple in Jerusalem. Micah's message is clear and direct; there is no room for misunderstanding. All levels and institutions of Judean society, including the temple, have become unjust, corrupt, and violent. Unless there are sincere and true repentance, judgment is both inevitable and immanent. Unfortunately, we know that God's people, apart perhaps from Hezekiah, did not repent and that disaster fell upon Jerusalem in 586 BC when the Babylonians looted the city and destroyed the temple.[21]

A WAKE-UP CALL FOR TODAY

The main point of the section is that the people of Israel, especially its leadership, have a responsibility to God and to others and that God will hold them accountable. The people of God must learn that with privilege comes responsibility, not only protection or special status. Being in a special relationship with God or being in a position of leadership does not make one immune to judgment. In fact, just the opposite is true, to whom more is given more will be required (see Luke 12:48; James 3:1). Micah's message is still as relevant for us as Christians today as it was back then for the people of Israel. God's plan for the world, his intention for the church, and what he expects of Christian leaders have not changed. Every Christian – especially leaders, pastors, and teachers – needs to examine very seriously his or her motivation, way of life, and responsibilities. There is no such thing as cheap grace. Appealing to the doctrine of election will not save us from God's judgment in this life nor on the Day of Judgment.

The problem with the leaders of Israel was that they were exploiting those under them, they were unjust, they were just interested in money and status, and they invented their own "revelations" pretending to be very virtuous. Unfortunately, we too often see the same attitudes and behavior in the church in Asia today. We need to recognize that the Asian church is no longer young, innocent, and pure. Dishonesty, corruption, and abuse – evils we commonly associate with the church in the West – have gained a foothold in many sections of the church in Asia. The reputation of Christianity has been marred in many cities, because of the bad behavior of its leaders. As Paul pointed out, quoting Isaiah 52:5, "God's name is blasphemed among the Gentiles because of you" (Rom 2:24). There should be thorough examination and serious repentance on the part of Christian leaders.

In particular, the leaders in Micah's time had five problems: (1) they invented their own theologies and ways of worshiping God (idolatry); (2) they were greedy for money (avarice); (3) they exploited and abused others for

---

21. Note the recently discovered seal of Hezekiah which depicts the story of his miraculous healing. See Robin Ngo, "King Hezekiah in the Bible: Royal Seal of Hezekiah Comes to Light," Bible History Daily (www.biblicalarchaeology.org); and Will Heilpern, "Biblical King's seal discovered in dump site" (edition.cnn.com).

personal gain (injustice); (4) they were not truthful about sin, but invented popular messages of peace (popularity); and (5) they linked God's favor to external privileges (affluence). What is our motivation for serving the Lord? We need to remember the sobering words of the Lord Jesus, "Not everyone who says to me, 'Lord, Lord,' will enter the kingdom of heaven, but only the one who does the will of my Father who is in heaven" (Matt 7:21).

Finally, we note that Samaria and Jerusalem were judged for the sin of their leaders. Living more than 2,000 years after Micah's prophecy, we have the benefit of hindsight. The prophecies about judgment were not theoretical threats or rhetorical devices to elicit passive reflection. Rather, the Assyrian destruction of Samaria and the Babylonian devastation of Jerusalem were all too real for the people of that time. Even today, archaeologists are uncovering arrow heads and black ash of intense fire in Samaria and Jerusalem as a reminder that the prophecies of judgment were indeed fulfilled as Micah warned. So too, churches have become ruins all over the West. Where there were once thriving Christian communities, today we have only empty cathedrals.

FALSE AND TRUE PROPHETS

One of the problems that Micah addressed was the presence of false prophets in Israel. In Micah 3:5, the prophet states, "This is what the Lord says: 'As for the prophets who lead my people astray, they proclaim 'peace' if they have something to eat, but prepare to wage war against anyone who refuses to feed them.'" False prophets appear throughout the history of the Old Testament, but it was especially around the time of the Babylonian exile that the canonical prophets highlighted the problem of deceptive prophets. Naturally, several questions arise. What is a false prophet? How can false prophets be distinguished from true prophets? And, is the issue regarding true and false prophets still relevant for the church today?

One of the foundational passages that deals with the problem of false prophets is Deuteronomy 18:15–22. Close analysis of the passage reveals three elements or tests that will enable God's people to distinguish true prophets from false ones. The first test relates to the call of the prophet, the second to the life of the prophet, and the third to the message of the prophet. It follows that true prophets will measure up to these three tests or criteria, false prophets will fail one or all of these tests. The first element that the text highlights is that the Lord "will raise up" the prophet and that the prophet will come "from among you – from your fellow Israelites" (Deut 18:15, 18). In other words, the Lord will call and commission the prophet; he or she will not presumptuously assume the position of prophet. Furthermore, the prophet will come from within Israel; he or she will be known by fellow Israelites and will grow up, as it were, within the traditions and community of Israel. The prophet will not be an outsider, a stranger, or a pagan. The second element that the text emphasizes is that the prophet will be "like Moses" (Deut 18:15, 18). This element relates to the character or life-style of the prophet – a prophet must mirror the character of Moses, the servant of God. The Pentateuch highlights that Moses was humble (Num 12:3), faithful (Num 12:7; compare Heb 3:5), and a man of prayer (Exod 24:12–18; 33:12–16; Num 11:1–2; 12:13), but especially that he was a suffering servant. For the sake of Israel and God's calling, Moses was prepared to stand up for his people risking his own life (Exod 2:12–15), he lived in an alien desert for 40 years (Exod 18:3; Acts 7:23, 30), he faced rebellion and opposition from others (Exod 14:10–12; 15:24; 16:2–3 17:2–3; Num 14:1–4; 16:1–14; 20:2–5; 21:4–5), and he carried the burden of shepherding the Israelites for 40 years in the desert (Exod 18:13–18; Num 11:14; 14:13–19; compare Heb 11:23–28). And, thirdly, the passage stresses that the prophet will bring the Lord's message by speaking only what the Lord commands (Deut 18:18). Therefore, the prophet will not fabricate messages, or proclaim ideas derived from people, dreams, or spirits.

It would have been relatively easy for the ancient Israelites to discern whether a prophet had been commissioned by God and stemmed from the fellowship of God's people. Likewise, the prophet's character would also have spoken for itself. Certainly, according to Deuteronomy 18:20, those who speak in the name of other gods were clearly false prophets. However, whereas it is easy to recognize pagan prophets, it is much more difficult to recognize false prophets who pretend to speak in the name of the Lord. Therefore, in verse 21, we read, "You may say to yourselves, 'How can we know when a message has not been spoken by the LORD?'" Since it will be more difficult to discern if the message of the prophet comes from the Lord, verse 22 deals specifically with the last test whether or not the prophet brings the Lord's message. Unfortunately, most Bible versions have not translated verse 22 correctly. The NIV, like most translations, reads, "If what a prophet proclaims in the name of the LORD does not take place or come true, that is a message the LORD has not spoken. That prophet has spoken presumptuously, so do not be alarmed." According to this translation, the test relates only to predictive prophecy, i.e. if the prophecy is not fulfilled, "does not take place or come true," then he or she is a false prophet. Instead, the Hebrew text actually (literally) reads, "That which the prophet speaks in the name of the LORD, and it is not the word, or it does not come about, that is the word which the LORD has not spoken. The prophet has spoken in presumption; do not be afraid of him." Note that the text presents two criteria for measuring the truthfulness of a prophecy. Firstly, the prophecy must "be the word," and secondly it must "come about." A careful analysis of "the word" indicates that the expression is used as a technical term for the Mosaic law as revealed in the book of Deuteronomy (Deut 4:10; 5:22; 6:6; 9:10; 10:2; 11:18; 12:28; 13:1; 24:18, 22; 28:14, 58; 29:1, 29; 30:14; 31:1, 12, 24; 32:44, 45–46). In fact, in the Hebrew Bible the title of Deuteronomy is "These are the Words" (Deut 1:1). Thus, the text deals with the two aspects of prophecy, forth-telling and fore-telling. If the prophet is forth-telling the word of the Lord, it must be the same or in accordance with what has already been revealed in the law of Moses. If the proclamation is different from the law of Moses, or about something else, then it is not a word from the Lord (see Deut 4:2; 12:32). On reflection, this criterion is quite logical, since God will not contradict himself. The second test relates to fore-telling or predictive prophecy. If the event is not fulfilled, the prophet has spoken presumptuously and is a false prophet. Of course, although Deuteronomy relates to subsequent prophets, according to the New Testament the passage is ultimately and perfectly fulfilled in Jesus (Matt 21:11; Mark 6:15; Luke 7:16, 26; John 1:21; 6:14; 7:40; Acts 3:22; 7:37).

Three characteristics of false prophets:
1) God did not call them nor sent them
2) They live immoral and avarice lives
3) They prophesy their own dreams and ideas (signs and wonders)

The three characteristics of true prophets:
1) The Lord called them and sent them
2) They live pure and honest lives (often persecuted)
3) They prophesy God's message (Messiah)

When we survey the description of false prophets in the Bible, we note that many prophets are false prophets, because they fail one of the three tests outlined above. They are not called by the Lord, have problematic lifestyles, and do not bring the Lord's message. Firstly, the canonical prophets castigate "false" prophets, because the Lord did not call them and did not send them, and yet they prophesy (Jer 14:14–15; 23:21). Secondly, they live immoral lives, being greedy, adulterous, and corrupt (Isa 27:7; Jer 6:13; 14:18; 23:10–15). And, thirdly, they preach their own ideas or dreams, which are nothing but illusions (Isa 30:10; Jer 2:8; 5:12–13; 23:11–32; Ezek 13:6, 9, 23). Their messages come from their own minds and are just about "smooth things" and "blessing" (Jer 23:16–17). Some even perform signs and wonders (Deut 13:1–5). On the other hand, true prophets, are called by the Lord, live pure and honest lives, often experience persecution, and most importantly faithfully proclaim God's message, which focuses on God's action in history and the promise of the coming Messiah (see Acts 10:43; Rev 19:10).

When we turn to the New Testament, we observe that the warning against false prophets is just as pronounced as it is in the Old Testament (Matt 7:15; 24:11; Mark 13:22; 2 Cor 11:13; Gal 2:4; 2 Pet 2:1–3; 1 John 4:1). So too, in church history, there have been many instances of people being led astray, Christians and non-Christians, by false prophets. Unfortunately, the problem is also very widespread in Asia. In China, sociologists estimate that Henan Province alone has more than 100 different cults and sects, and it is often said that there are 330 million gods in India. But more disturbingly, when we apply the three Old Testament tests for discerning between true and false prophets to preachers and teachers in the church today, many are quite problematic. Their calling is obscure and they have no authoritative validation by church leadership. And, instead of holiness and simplicity, their lifestyles are characterized by immorality and greed. Furthermore, most conspicuously, their messages focus on "smooth things" or "new revelations" rather than the gospel about Jesus. This problem is so serious that in the Old Testament false prophets were to be put to death and in the New Testament they were to be excommunicated from the church. In fact, Micah traces the source of Israel's numerous sins back to the feet of the prophets. In general, they had all become remiss in their roles, having fallen in love with the things of the world. They were supposed to be watchmen and guardians of the covenant, the last defense against apostasy, and yet they had become God's biggest problem and obstacle in calling his people and the world back to himself (Jer 23:36–40). The book of Micah highlights this problem for the church today.

MICAH 4-5:
THE MESSAGE OF RESTORATION

MICAH 4

After Micah exposed Israel's sin – the Message of Destruction – he comes with an amazing announcement of hope and salvation – the Message of Restoration. There is a dramatic shift in mood in chapters 4 to 5 in comparison with chapters 1 to 3. Whereas we hear mostly of Israel's iniquity and God's judgment in chapters 1 to 3, chapters 4 to 5 shine with confidence and light. The contrast between the fortunes of God's people in the first section and second section of the book of Micah cannot be greater. In the first section, God is the Lord of judgment, in the second section he is portrayed as the Lord of hope. "In a breathtaking shift, Micah moves from the dismantling of the old Jerusalem to the rebuilding of the new."[1]

Micah is moving from a picture of Israel's past failure to the bright future of Israel's restoration. God has not abandoned his people, nor his plan for the world; rather, despite their sins, God will yet bring about a most glorious salvation for all people. God has not discarded his plan of salvation history. Instead, we see exactly the opposite happening, it is becoming ever more glorious. The most prominent theme in Micah is not about judgment, but about restoration.[2] Two of the greatest and most well-known prophecies in the Old Testament are in this section: the restored Jerusalem and the ruler from Bethlehem.

Commentators have struggled to provide a coherent interpretation of chapters 4 to 5 because of the diversity of material. They have often seen contradictions and the hand of many editors at work in this section. For example, some scholars placed the social context of the oracles in the exilic (James L. Mayes) or post-exilic period (Bruce Vawter, Hans Wolff, D. P. Cole, Francis I. Andersen and David N. Freedman), and some have perceived different and opposing voices within the material (Juan I. Alfaro). However, as we have already argued in the introduction, there is no compelling evidence to support any of these suggestions. On the other hand, we may derive at a coherent

---
1. Waltke, *Micah: An Introduction and Commentary*, 166.
2. Contra Smith, *Micah-Malachi*, 10.

interpretation of the section within a pre-exilic context in accordance with the historical, narrative, and canonical contexts.

It appears that the main underlying reason for assigning much of the material to a post-586 BC date is the reluctance of scholars to accept the possibility of predictive prophecy. However, such a predisposition does not adhere with good scholarship, since it is not willing to consider seriously all the data or all possibilities; the presupposition about the impossibility of predictive prophecy has already determined the results. Even if one were to dismiss divine orchestration of historical events, it does not preclude the possibility that some predictions about the future may come true by accident. Undoubtedly, there lies a history of transmission behind the text of the book of Micah and we have argued that the book underwent a complex process of redaction. However, reconstructing that compositional history, distinguishing between the core and secondary material, earlier and later redaction, and dating such levels to specific time-frames are more or less impossible. It is difficult to derive at any level of certainty regarding these questions. In fact, the diverse reconstructions of scholars demonstrate that this kind of work is not "scientific" at all – if we require that scientific inquiry must be based on evidence and a methodology that provides the same results irrespective of the researcher. Rather, the divergent reconstructions of Micah's compositional history illustrate that they depend on the proclivities and creative imaginations of the constructors.

The second reason for assigning much of the material in chapters 4 to 5 to a post-586 BC date is the disparity between the Message of Judgment of the previous section and the Message of Restoration in these subsequent chapters. However, we also do not accept that this argument is a definitive reason for attributing the sections to two different prophets. It is not inconceivable that a prophet of judgment may also announce future times of restoration. In fact, it is very likely that prophecies of judgment will be followed with prophecies of salvation. After all, what would be the point of censuring bad behavior and announcing judgment if there is no possibility of repentance? True prophets, as opposed to false prophets, are those who have been called by the Lord and who announce the message of the Lord, whatever that may be. In other words, there are good reasons for arguing that the book of Micah stems from the prophetic activities of the eighth century prophet Micah and contains a coherent message. Of course, Micah's prophecies or the book of Micah would have undergone a process of redaction over many years until it reached its current shape, but it is now impossible to reconstruct that process.

Figure 10. Statue in front of United Nations building in New York of man beating a sword into a plowshare. It was created by Evgeniy Vuchetich and donated to the UN by the USSR in 1959. (Neptuul/Wikimedia Commons)[3]

4:1–5 An Oracle of Global Peace

The Message of Restoration begins with perhaps the grandest vision in the Old Testament about the future of the world. It is hard to find another passage in Scripture – apart from the book of Revelation – that presents such a splendid vision. It has inspired many people over the centuries to work for a better and more peaceful world; the sword being beaten into a ploughshare has even been chosen as the emblem of the United Nations (see Figure 10). Indeed, the vision expresses God's plan for the world and the goal of salvation history. Few other worldviews come close to the exhilaration and hope that

---

3. Image: Let Us Beat Swords into Plowshares, sculpture by Yevgeny Vuchetich. Photo by Neptuul via https://commons.wikimedia.org/wiki/File:Schwerter_zu_Pflugscharen_-_Jewgeni_Wutschetitsch_-_Geschenk_der_Sowjetunion_an_die_UNO_-_1959.jpg

are presented here. However, one should never forget the historical context of the vision. Amazingly, it comes after the message of judgment and destruction of the northern kingdom. The prophet Micah was not an ivory tower theologian who lived in comfort, but was a person who had come through all kinds of anguish and travail. He had seen with his own eyes the demolition of Samaria and had felt the grief of lost hope. And yet, the contrast between the faith expressed in the vision here and the reality described in chapters 1 to 3 cannot be greater. To what can we attribute such optimism and hope? The answer is obvious. Micah received a vision from the Lord and mixed that vision with faith.

It is difficult to classify the vision according to the standard categories used to analyze prophetic literature. It is more than a salvation oracle, which is related to a specific historical context, and often directly addresses the people of God with a specific command like "do not fear." Andersen calls it an "apocalypse,"[4] but many features of later apocalyptic literature are absent. As von Rad and Wildberger have argued, the language is neither ancient nor late and is similar to many pre-exilic Psalms of Zion (e.g. Pss 46, 48, 87), and, as far as we can detect, it fits well with Micah's historical and literary context.[5] Perhaps, it is best to describe the passage as an eschatological vision of global devotion and peace. It is "eschatological" because it relates to "the last days," and it is a "vision" because it aims to inspire hope. There is a brilliant juxtaposition of parallelism, alliteration, and allusion in the text that encourages careful contemplation.

Before we examine the content of the vision, we need to comment briefly on its relationship with Isaiah 2:1–5 where the same prophecy appears. Traditionally, writers thought that the passage originated with Micah and that Isaiah borrowed it from him. More recently critical scholars have postulated that the passage was composed after the return from the exile in an Isaianic context and that it was later incorporated into the book of Micah with some minor changes. According to Limburg, the text in Micah is later, its Hebrew is smoother, and the text is longer.[6] However, some still argue that it originated with Micah.[7] Several scholars also suggested that the vision was "common

---

4. See Francis I. Andersen and David Noel Freedman. *Micah: A New Translation with Introduction and Commentary*, AB (New York: Doubleday, 2000), 397.
5. Gerhard von Rad and H. Wildberger have argued that the language of the vision is very similar to many pre-exilic Psalms of Zion (e.g. Pss 46, 48, 87). The origins of the Zion tradition lie before the 8th century, see J. J. M. Roberts, and "The Davidic Origin of the Zion Tradition," *JBL* 92 (1973), 329–344.
6. Limburg, *Hosea-Micah. Interpretation: A Bible Commentary for Teaching and Preaching*, 180.
7. For example, see Hillers, *Micah: A Commentary on the Book of the Prophet Micah*, 52–53.

property" and that both Isaiah and Micah incorporated it into their respective traditions.[8] As these proposals demonstrate, scholars are far from solving this mystery. There is simply not enough data or evidence to come to any firm conclusion about the relationship between the two passages. We may only note that the occurrence of the passage in two canonical prophets – both occurring at key literary junctures – underscores its importance.

As already inferred above, the conjunction "and" in the Hebrew, which is regrettably not translated in many English versions, link the vision closely with the preceding section. So too, the key expression "mountain of the LORD's temple" in the Hebrew connects the passage to Micah 3:12. It is clear that the book of Micah was edited and must be read as a coherent whole. Only then will one understand the meaning of the details. Out of God's judgment and destruction, something new is going to spring. The judgment of destruction (chapters 1–3) is not the only message of the book of Micah. In fact, it is only the beginning; it lays the foundation of the central part of the book. There are going to be renewal and salvation, not just for the people of God, but for all nations. God has not given up on his plan to bless the world through his people, but is committing himself with renewed vigor to accomplish it. It is hard to overestimate the joy that this image of a restored Zion and global peace, after the experience of destruction, would have brought to Micah and his companions. In fact, restoration after destruction, or life after death, is a very prominent motif throughout the Bible. We observe this paradox in Genesis 3 where grace and life follow rebellion and death, in the flood where a new community emerges after the deluge, and in the great saga of Jonah where the Gentiles are saved after "the death and resurrection" of the prophet. This principle reminds us of the words of Habakkuk 3:2, "in wrath you remember mercy" (my own translation), and, of course, is nowhere more pronounced than in the death and resurrection of Jesus.

The expression "in the last days" is common Old Testament eschatological terminology that refers to an unspecified time in the future (see Mic 2:4). According to Anderson, "In Deuteronomistic-prophetic usage the phrase in the last days refers specifically to restoration after a calamity."[9] The plural term "days" indicates that the prophecy will not be fulfilled in an instant – in one day – but will involve a process of time. The following three parallel lines make this process clearer. Firstly, there will be a restoration of the Lord's house, i.e.

---

8. For example, see B. Vawter, *Amos, Hosea, Micah, with an Introduction to Classical Prophecy* (Wilmington, DE: Michael Glazier, 1981), 149.
9. Andersen, *Micah: A New Translation with Introduction and Commentary*, 401.

the temple. The Hebrew verb "will be established" (*kûn*) can also mean "to re-establish" or "to restore" (see Num 21:27; 2 Chr 29:35). In the future, the mountain of the Lord's temple will gain more prominence on earth than all other mountains, and all people will stream to it. "Mountain" is a common image in biblical poetry and must be carefully interrupted within its context as it can signify different things. In connection with the temple, the image here refers to the teaching, worship, and faith that relates to the God of Israel. In the ancient world, most temples were built on mountains since people believed that mountains were the abode of the gods, or were closer to heaven than the lower plains. Micah announces that in the future the devotion relating to the God of Israel will become the most prominent worldview or faith in the world. In the context of Israel's defeat and its insignificance in the world of that time, the prophecy is extraordinarily courageous and optimistic. Likewise, it is important to observe that Mount Zion is not particularly high – it is not really a mountain by our standards – nor does it have any noteworthy physical feature that distinguishes it from other hills (see Figure 11). In fact, even among the hills of Israel it is quite small and ordinary, and the surrounding hills like the Mount of Olives is higher in elevation. There is only one feature that makes Mount Zion different from all other mountains, and that is, as the next verses will highlight, the word of the Lord.

**Figure 11. Jerusalem is surrounded by hills.
The Mount of Olives lies in the background**

Micah 4-5: The Message of Restoration

Verse 2 expands on the last line of verse 1. Gentiles will encourage one another to do three things: to go up to the mountain of the Lord, to learn his ways, and to walk according to his paths. One may argue that the verb "go up" (*'alah*), which occurs frequently in the Exodus narrative, does not only denote the physical ascent to the mountain on which the temple is built, but also the aspiration to seek higher things or to move spiritually closer to God. The verb often carries this nuance (see Exod 19:3, 24; 24:1, 12; 32:30) and may indicate a change in status (see Pss 30:3; 40:3). The reason given for the nations' pilgrimage to the temple is truly amazing; it is so that the Lord may teach them "his ways." It is easy to understand that some Gentiles may want to come and inquire about the faith of the Jews, but here the text announces that the LORD (Yahweh) himself will teach the Gentiles. It does not only mean that the Gentile nations have become part of the covenant family, but also that they will enjoy a privileged position before the Lord. In the Old Testament only Moses (Exod 4:12, 15) and some choice individuals (Pss 25:8, 12; 27:11; 32:8; 86:11; 119:33, 102) had the privilege of being directly taught by God. It was the duty of Moses, and then later the duty of the priests, to teach the Israelites what God taught Moses (Exod 24:12; Lev 10:11; Deut 4:44–45; 5:1–5; 17:10–11).[10] Here in Micah a new status is envisaged for the Gentile nations that is even more elevated than that which the Israelites enjoyed during Micah's time (Ps 47:10).[11] The Lord's instruction will be for a practical purpose, viz. "so that we may walk in his paths." Consequently, in verse 3 we note that the nations will subject themselves to God's authority and kingship, resulting in world peace. The last line in verse 2 gives another reason for this dramatic change. The "coming in" of the nations will be the result of the "going out" of the Lord's word. The picture is very similar to the last vision in Isaiah 66 where the proclamation of God's glory among the nations will result in the coming of many to Jerusalem (Isa 66:18–21).

The text is also rich with paronomasia and suggestive imagery. In verse 1, the word "peoples" (*amim*) sounds like "water" (*mayim*) in Hebrew, and so people can "stream" or "flow" to Jerusalem (which will truly be miraculous since Jerusalem is on a hill!). Furthermore, we note that in Hebrew the law (*torah*) is based on the same root as the verb "to teach" (*yarah*), which suggests that the dissemination of God's teaching among the nations will draw the

---

10. Later, according to Jeremiah, this divine instruction will be one of the signs of the new covenant (Jer 31:31–34).
11. It is interesting to note that the LXX hides this new status for Gentiles by translating the Hebrew as "they shall show us his way."

nations to receive further teaching from God. And, finally, since water is often used as a symbol of the law (it gives life) in the Bible (see Ps 1:3; Isa 55:10–11; Jer 17:8–13; Ezek 19:10; 34:18; 47:1–12), it is interesting to note that the verbal root for the word "teaching" (*yarah*) has a homonym that means "to give drink" or "to rain" (see Hos 6:3). The Lord's teaching will be the catalyst for new life and peace in the world. Therefore, according to the passage, God's word will be the essential element that sets Jerusalem apart from other places. Terms suggestive of natural imagery creates a poetic world that is rich with spiritual meaning.

Verses 3 and 4 picture the result that will follow from the ingathering of the Gentiles into the covenant community of God's people. There will be new righteousness and justice, since God will be ruler and his standards will prevail. It is instructive to comment on the main verb used in the first line of verse 3, which is usually translated "to judge" (*shaphat*), depicting the activity of a judge. However, the verb may also mean "to rule," depicting the activity of a king. It may be better in the context here to translate the term "to rule," which is broader in scope than "to judge." Micah may have decided to use this term since he was particularly interested in justice. Hence, in the context of Micah, the meaning is, "And he will rule with justice among many peoples."[12] The injustices described in chapters 1 and 2 will disappear. There will be a dramatic downturn in the arms industry. Military colleges will close their doors, since there will be no more war. Rather, more resources will be invested in agriculture and the care of the environment. As a result, individuals or the common folk will have property, sufficient means for living, security, and leisure to enjoy family, friends, and the enrichment of life. Indeed, this vision provides the quintessential example of Old Testament eschatological hope and is closely related to the messianic kingdom (see Gen 49:8–12; Ps 72; Isa 9:1–7; 11:1–16; Dan 2:35–45; 7:13–14). The image of everyone sitting "under their own vine and under their own fig tree" denotes security, prosperity, and peace. It recalls the situation under the kingdom of Solomon (1 Kgs 4:25), which was very different from the time of Hezekiah (2 Kgs 18:31).[13] But, unusually, this typical Hebraic phrase that describes Israel's ideal future (Isa 36:16; Zech 3:10) is here used to describe the future of the Gentile nations.

In light of the vision, the final verse outlines the two alternatives or two choices before the peoples of the world. It presents a realistic assessment of the

---

12. The Hebrew preposition *byn* can be translated "among," as in the Septuagint.
13. Also see Walter Brueggemann, "Vine and Fig Tree: A Case Study in Imagination and Criticism," *CBQ* 43 (1981), 188–204.

Micah 4–5: The Message of Restoration

future as well as the confidence of Micah and his community amidst pluralism and turbulence. On the one hand, many will continue to follow their own gods and desires. But, on the other hand, the believing community will renew its determination to be hopeful and faithful to the Lord. Evidently, despite the reassuring prospect of global peace, there are always going to be people, and perhaps even nations, who will not be convinced. We disagree with Alfaro who has seen a contradiction between verse 2 where nations will come to the Lord and verse 5 where nations will continue to follow their own gods.[14] Prophetic speech is poetry and, therefore, one should avoid literalism and ascertain the main intention the author wanted to convey through the use of parallelism and imagery. Ancient readers were not naïve, but had sophisticated literary appreciation. Often, in Scripture, words like "all" or "none," according to the context, mean "many" or "some." Rather, the verse keeps an unlimited optimism in check, and highlights the need for the faithful to remain resolute amidst an idolatrous environment.

The main question to be answered is, "When will this vision be fulfilled?" When we turn to the New Testament, the answer becomes clear. Many Christian interpreters have taken these verses to refer to the time after the second coming of the Lord Jesus. The vision will certainly be perfectly fulfilled after the return of the Lord and may be read in conjunction with Revelation 21 and 22. However, this vision, also relates to the first coming of the Lord Jesus and our present time; it does not just apply to the future return of the Lord. Firstly, the eschatological vision of the Old Testament about the events of the "latter days" or the "last day" is fulfilled in the new era of salvation inaugurated with the first coming of the Lord Jesus Christ. The "latter days" of the Old Testament have become "today" in the New Testament (see Luke 4:21; 5:26; 13:32; 19:5, 9; 23:43; Acts 2:17–18; Heb 3:7, 13, 15; 4:7). Even though the New Testament writers anticipate that the Lord will return again in bodily form (Acts 11:9–11; Thess 5:2; 2 Thess 2:2; 2 Pet 3:10), the anticipated messianic kingdom has already arrived (Matt 11:2–5, 12; 12:28; Mark 9:1; Luke 17:21; Rom 14:17; 1 Cor 4:20; 2 Cor 5:17; 1 John 2:8). However, the kingdom does not come all at once, but grows like a mustard seed into a tree or expands its influence in the world like yeast through a lump of dough (Mark 13:26–32; Matt 13:33; see also Mark 4:26–27; Dan 2:31–45). In other words, the global vision of peace envisaged by Micah does not come suddenly, but is a process that will begin with the coming of the

---

14. Alfaro, *Justice and Loyalty: A Commentary on the Book of Micah*, 43.

Messiah. This New Testament interpretation of the coming of the kingdom as a process ties in well with the multiple or progressive fulfillment of prophecy. Secondly, in the New Testament the key terms of "Zion," "Jerusalem," the "house of the Lord" (i.e. the temple), and the "way" are regularly applied to the events, places, and movements surrounding Jesus and his followers. Jesus and his disciples (i.e. the church) become the new temple (John 2:21; 1 Cor 3:16; 2 Cor 6:16; Eph 2:21), and even Gentile believers are described with the labels "Jerusalem," "Zion," and "Israel" (see Gal 4:26; 6:16; Heb 12:22; Rom 9:6; 11:26; 1 Pet 2:9). One of the earliest expressions used to refer to the followers of Jesus is the term "Way" (Acts 9:2). And we also believe that the "mountain" points to the cross which was set up on Mount Zion, particularly at the place called "Golgotha" (Mark 15:22; see also John 12:31). Therefore, New Testament writers habitually use the terms of the vision to describe features in the life of Jesus and the Gentile church. Thirdly, several other Old Testament prophecies that are closely related to the vision presented here are interpreted by the New Testament authors as being fulfilled in their current time. For example, in Acts the eschatological outpouring of the Spirit in the "last days" (Acts 2:16–21, see also Joel 2:28–30), the powerful reign of the Messiah (Acts 2:34–35, compare Ps 110:1; Acts 4:25–26, compare Ps 2:1–2), and the ingathering of the Gentiles happen in the experience of the church (Acts 15:15–18, compare Amos 9:11–12). So too, in his Epistle to the Romans, Paul interpreted prophecies related to the future blessing of the Gentiles as being fulfilled in the church (Rom 9:25–26, compare Hos 1:10; 2:23; Rom 10:18–21, compare Deut 32:21 and Isa 65:1–2; Rom 15:9–12, compare Ps 18:49; Ps 117:1; Isa 11:10). Paul also related prophecies about the future restoration of Israel to the current time (Rom 11:26–27, compare Isa 27:9; 59:20). Therefore, according to the New Testament perspective, this prophecy in Micah 4 is in the process of being fulfilled with the spread of the gospel and the growth of God's kingdom across the world. One should remember, of course, that prophetic language is poetic or symbolic and often goes beyond crude literalism,[15] i.e. more than a merely physical restoration of the temple is in view. Even though the temple was rebuilt after the return of the Jews in 538 BC, the reality of the second temple fell far short of what was envisaged here (see Hag 2:3). According to the vision, the future of Israel will far outshine its history; there will be a new obedience or a new heart (see Deut 4:30; Hos 3:5) and the whole world will come to be blessed.

---

15. Limburg, *Hosea-Micah. Interpretation: A Bible Commentary for Teaching and Preaching*, 181.

MICAH 4-5: THE MESSAGE OF RESTORATION

A BRIGHT FUTURE FOR ASIA

Over the last century many parts of Asia have been devastated by war and today Asians continue to experience the ravages of violence, corruption, exploitation, and pollution. The new arms race in Asia does not provide much hope for a peaceful future. In many places, Christians suffer exploitation and the church is ravaged by corrupt and egoistic clergy. However, the book of Micah has a very encouraging message for Asian Christians today that will inspire hope and generate change. Micah's striking vision of global peace may re-invigorate Christian life and inspire ministry. Indeed, Christians can be assured of God's victory and live with confidence and hope. The church in Asia may again experience restoration and see millions of people eager to become followers of Jesus. According to Waltke, readers must see the vision, hear the words, and then reflect long upon it.[1] Its images were watchfully painted for the eye, its words were carefully scripted for the ear, and its poetic arrangements were prudently crafted for the heart.

For Christians, there are three main points for application. Firstly, Christians need to continue to attend church, "not giving up meeting together, as some are in the habit of doing, but encouraging one another – and all the more as you see the Day approaching" (Heb 10:25). Despite many past failings, the church is the redeemed community of the Lord and is the hope of the world. In Asia, often, it is only in the church where there are still truth and sincerity. But not only should Christians continue to go to church, they should also invite and encourage their neighbors to join them. Secondly, Christians need to come with a renewed interest to learn from the Bible to understand God's plan for the church and for the world. The Bible often says that God's people are destroyed for a lack of knowledge (see Hos 4:6; Isa 5:13) and are easily led astray (see Gal 1:6; Eph 2:14). Therefore, Christians should make a new commitment to enroll in Jesus' school of discipleship, to understand the gospel, and to sit at the Lord's feet to hear his voice and be enriched with true spiritual food. And, thirdly, perhaps most importantly, Christians need to walk according to God's word. There needs to be a change in attitude, values, and especially lifestyle. Christians must embrace lives of self-denial and cross-bearing, and should stand out in the crowd for their humility, honesty, generosity, kindness, gentleness, and righteousness. In this way, Christians will become the light and salt of Asia, darkness and decay will decrease, and many societies will be transformed.[2]

There have been many attempts in church history to establish an ideal Christian community on earth, inspired by Old Testament prophecies such as Micah 4:1-5. In Acts 2:42–47 the early community of believers centered around the teaching of the apostles, lived harmoniously together, met everyone's needs, and had everything in common. This serene community at Pentecost when people from all nations gathered in Jerusalem was the beginning of the fulfillment of this prophecy. Throughout the Middle Ages many Christians, following the example of Anthony of Egypt (251–346), set up monastic communities in remote places in order to escape the corruption of the world. Perhaps the most well-known example is that of Francis of Assisi (1181–1228), who inspired thousands with his simplicity and devoted service to the poor. After the Reformation, many Protestants also established communities for the promotion of piety, equality, and brotherly love. Philipp Spener (1635–1705), one of the founders of Pietism, established small groups which met for devotional readings, prayer, and spiritual encouragement. Count von Zinzendorf (1700–1760) organized religious refugees from Moravia into a community on his estate, which became known as the Moravian Church. The community emphasized the "religion of the heart," the unity of all Christians, mission, and music. Many Puritans, after fleeing persecution in England, also tried to set up societies based on the idea of a Holy Commonwealth in the new American colonies. In the 19th century there were hundreds of Christian communities in the US attempting to establish utopian societies on earth. In China, the Jesus Family founded by Jing Dianying in Shandong Province (耶穌家庭 yesu jiating) – a Christian utopian movement – espoused the same ideals. However, although these attempts achieved some good, in the end they all failed to establish peace in the world – some even led to bitter disappointment due to corruption and abuse. Nevertheless, these examples provide small glimpses into God's intention for the future and remind us that ultimately the ideal society will be achieved only when Jesus himself returns to judge those who disobey the gospel and to bring his kingdom to perfect completion. Therefore, Christians in Asia may pray with confidence that they too may experience glimpses, or foretastes, of this vision in their own churches and communities.

---

1. Waltke, *Micah: An Introduction and Commentary*, 166.
2. It is interesting to note John Calvin's disappointment when he reflected on the implementation of this vision in his own time. He wrote in his commentary on Micah that "though the Gospel in many parts is clearly preached, yet discords and contentions do not cease; we may also see that rapacity, ambition, and insatiable avarice, greatly prevail; and hence arise contentions and bloody wars." Calvin thinks that the reason for this is because "the number of the faithful is small, and the greater part despise and reject the Gospel, . . . the doctrine of the Gospel strikes root hardly in one out of a hundred." In *Commentary on Jonah, Micah, Nahum*, 157.

Micah 4-5: The Message of Restoration

4:6–12 God Will Gather His Remnant

This oracle about God gathering his remnant is a continuation of the message about restoration commenced in verses 1 to 5. Accordingly, the Masoretic scribes inserted a section division only after verse 7, linking verses 6 and 7 to the preceding vision.[16] The verses emphasize that God will cause the gathering of people – his remnant – and, as implied in the preceding vision, it will be a divine or miraculous event. "In that day" covers the same general period as indicated by the expression "in the last days" in verse 1. The verb "to gather" (*Qal*) often indicates calling people together for a specific task or summoning people to congregate for worship (Num 11:16, 22, 24; Deut 16:13; Josh 24:1), whereas the verb "to assemble" (*Pi'el*) denotes a concerted effort to restore those who have been scattered. The verbal sequence was already used in Micah 2:12. It recalls the words of Deuteronomy 30:3–4, which promise a return to the land after exile, if Israel repents. God's gathering his scattered people is a common refrain in other parts of Scripture, but it is significant to note that the gathering sometimes also incorporates the coming of Gentiles to Jerusalem (see Pss 102:22; 106:47; 107:3; Amos 9:12; Isa 11:12; 40:11; 43:5, 9; 49:6–12; 54:7; 56:8; 60:4, 7; 66:18).

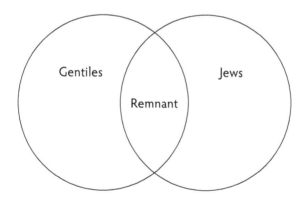

Figure 12

Therefore, in our analysis of the text, this second oracle of the Message of Restoration provides a further explanation of the identity of those coming to Jerusalem in verses 1 to 2. They are now also identified as the remnant; in

---

16. The Masoretic scribes were the Jewish rabbis who edited the Hebrew Bible during the Middle Ages.

other words, there is an overlap between the nations coming to Jerusalem in verse 1 and the remnant that is gathered in verses 6 to 7. In the future, the separation between Israel and the Gentiles will disappear; there will be a union of Jews and Gentiles to become God's remnant (see Figure 12). Moreover, the verses describe this "gathering" or "remnant" as "the lame" and as those whom God has "brought to grief" or the "afflicted" (see Zeph 3:19–20). Again, the prophet uses his words carefully to invoke the memory of Israel's stories and experience, describing the future in language of the past. "The lame" reminds the reader of the story of Jacob, who after he had struggled with God, became limp (Gen 32:31–32). Thus, a real personal cost was involved in changing from "Jacob" to "Israel." "The afflicted" refers to the ones who have experienced suffering, and perhaps even the judgment of God. It is the same root for the word (*ra'*) used in Micah 1:12 and 2:3 which describes the judgment that God will bring upon his people. In other words, paradoxically, restoration will be the outcome of destruction, and gathering will be the result of scattering (see also Ps 119:67, 71); the "lame" will become the "remnant," and the "afflicted" will become the "strong nation."[17] The language with respect to the remnant describes ordinary people who try to be faithful to the Lord within a chaotic, oppressive, and ungodly society.

We have already come across the concept of the remnant in Micah 2:12, but it now becomes much more prominent in the Message of Restoration (Mic 4:7; 5:7–8) and incorporates both Jews and Gentiles. God is going to use the ones who carry the scars of struggle and affliction – Jew and Gentile – to be the building blocks of his new city and kingdom. As mentioned in the introduction, Micah is not just calling God's people back to covenant faithfulness; he is also proclaiming a remarkable new message about future restoration that will include Gentiles and especially the afflicted. In fact, one wonders what impact the resettlement of Samaria by Gentiles would have had on the theological reflection of the prophets (compare 2 Kgs 17:24–41). Although the Gentiles imported their own religions to Samaria, many also adopted the faith of Israel.

All this will take place because the Lord will be king and reign over his people in Jerusalem. The last eight words of verse 7 stand right in the middle of the book of Micah and capture its central hope: there will be restoration

---

17. Waltke writes, "According to the New Testament the church has become the strong nation in view here (1 Pet 2:9–10)." In *Micah: An Introduction and Commentary*, 176.

for God's people when the Lord establishes his kingdom.[18] There is criticism of the contemporary kings of Israel who reigned from the "stronghold (i.e. the Ophel) of the daughter of Zion" (compare Micah 1:1) (see Figure 13). The kings of the northern kingdom are probably no more, and those of the southern kingdom cannot do much to curtail injustice and idolatry. Like their northern counterparts, they are powerless to avert destruction and the coming exile. God's people need a new king that will be able to inaugurate the reign of peace described in verses 1 to 4. The resolution to the current crisis is given here; the Lord himself will come to his people in order to be king in their midst. The sentiment of the text echoes the Song of Moses after Israel's great deliverance from the Egyptians at the Sea of Reeds (Exod 15:18; compare Ps 146:10) and is similar to the language about the Lord's coming reign in the prophecies of Isaiah (Isa 40:9–11; 52:7–10; 61:1–4). The Lord himself will come to bring about the eschatological vision of global peace. The image behind the language of gathering and rule was that of the king as shepherd of his people, which was the prevalent understanding of ideal kingship in the Ancient Near East.

Figure 13. The Ophel in the City of David, Jerusalem

---

18. In the Leningrad Codex the book of Micah contains 1405 words. If we discard the 18 words in the title or superscript (Mic 1:1), a break at Micah 4:7 divides the book in two equal halves.

There have been several suggestions regarding the identity of the person addressed by the pronoun "you" in verse 8. Since kingship belongs to that person, it could be a reference to God who may be considered to be the "watchtower of the flock" and "stronghold of the Daughter of Zion." Another possibility is that the returning exiles are in view here, but it will then be difficult to explain the difference between "the watchtower of the flock" and the people in general as they are separate entities. Another suggestion is that the remnant, as a sub-entity within the people of God, is being addressed; a faithful remnant will be the catalyst of blessing to all the people of God. A fourth option is that the prophet Micah may be the one addressed, since as a prophet he served as a "watcher" or "guard" over the people of God (see Hos 9:8; Ezek 3:17) and through God's word exercised the power of the coming kingdom. However, the best explanation in our opinion is that verse 8 is a declaration about the future deliverer and his coming kingdom. The sequence of verses 7 and 8 is the same as the sequence in chapter 2 verses 12 and 13. After the prophet described God gathering his remnant, he portrayed their deliverer. Verse 8 is a rhetorical address to the coming ruler, an anticipation of the Messiah, who will be more clearly identified in Micah 5:2–3. Other canonical texts similarly attribute kingship to the coming deliverer of Israel (Isa 9:7; 11:1–5; Dan 7:14). The "former dominion" probably refers to the glorious power Israel enjoyed under the reigns of David and Solomon. Therefore, in verse 9 the prophet encourages his dejected compatriots to lift up their heads in anticipation of the arrival of their true king. It does not necessarily imply, as some have suggested, that there was no king at the time and that we hear the lament of the exilic community. Rather, the kings were powerless to affect change and protect Judah from her enemies, and the counselors were confused and did not know what to advise (see Jer 8:19). In other words, there is no real king in Jerusalem; even Hezekiah is more concerned about his own well-being than the future of God's people (see Isa 39:5–8). We may imagine that a group of like-minded people often met with Micah to commiserate over the current state of Judah and also to anticipate a brighter future. Micah compares their anguish with a woman in labor, probably the greatest pain a human can endure, but which is accompanied with the expectation of new life. Therefore, these compatriots are very distressed over Judah's situation, nonetheless preserve hope for restoration.

But according to verse 10, the agony will become worse before it becomes better. The image of a woman in labor is extended; there will be more pain since Judah, like the northern kingdom, will be exiled into Babylon. However, the exile will be followed by a great deliverance; from Babylon God will redeem his people. The same image is used by the prophet Isaiah when he likens the anguish of the Day of the Lord with the pain of childbirth (Isa 13:8) as well as the joy of childbirth (Isa 66:8–9). Jesus also picks up the metaphor in John 16:21–22 and applies it to the experience of the disciples during the time of his crucifixion and resurrection. The verb "to rescue" is used with respect to the exodus from Egypt (Exod 18:10) and also in the Psalms to denote deliverance from sin and guilt (Pss 39:10; 51:14; 79:9). The verb "to redeem" literally means "to act as a kinsman" and recalls the responsibility one has as a family member (Lev 25:25; Num 5:8; and especially see Ruth 2:20; 3:9, 12; 4:1–14). In view of the covenant relationship, God redeems Israel from Egypt (Exod 6:6; 15:3) and from exile in Babylon (Isa 41:14; 43:1, 14; 44:6, 22–24; 47:4; 48:17; 49:7, 26; 54:4, 8). Therefore, paradoxically, the exile does not mean defeat for God's people, but just the opposite; it will be the catalyst of a great deliverance. Alfaro, thus, perceptively understands the main theme of these verses as "salvation through suffering."[19] This prophecy about exile was fulfilled when the Babylonians destroyed Jerusalem and burned the temple in 586 BC. So too, the prophecy about deliverance from exile was initially fulfilled in 538 BC when the new Persian emperor, Cyrus, allowed the Jews to return to the land of Israel.

Several scholars have speculated that the words, "you will go to Babylon," prove that it is a late oracle written after the Babylonian exile in 586 BC. Similarly, others conjectured that the initial "Assyria," the empire that threatened Judah in the eighth century, was replaced by "Babylon" after the captivity of the southern kingdom. For example, Kaufmann supposed that this is "one of the few instances in the whole corpus of prophecy of a genuine revision in light of later events."[20] However, one should not uncritically accept this conjecture, since the evidence for such argumentation is quite weak. Firstly, if theism is not discounted from the range of possible worldviews, then the feasibility of predictive prophecy must be accepted. Secondly, there is no textual evidence from the manuscript tradition that the text was altered. Thirdly, Babylon already existed at the time and was an important city-state, and Isaiah already predicted a Babylonian invasion (see Isa 39; 2 Kgs 20:12–19). And, fourthly, those who surmise that this prophecy was written after the event must explain why other parts of the book of Micah were not altered similarly. Apart from

---

19. Alfaro, *Justice and Loyalty: A Commentary on the Book of Micah*, 52.
20. Y. Kaufmann, *The Religion of Israel*. Abridged and translated, Moshe Greenberg (Chicago: University of Chicago Press, 1960), 352.

this one reference, there is nothing in the book that relates any detail about what we know to have occurred around the time of the Babylonian exile. If the text was open to modification and an editor wanted to create predictive prophecies after the events had taken place, surely he would have done a better job. Rather, we know that the book of Micah existed some thirty years before the fall of Jerusalem in 586 BC, which implies that it had already attained some fixed form by then (see Jer 26:18). Thus, it is not likely that someone would have changed the text intentionally.

Verses 11 to 12 underscore the paradox of Israel's coming experience, something that is beyond the understanding of her enemies. Israel's enemies are determined in plotting her downfall. They think they have gained a big victory through defeating her and carrying her off into exile. However, they are not aware that the defeat of Israel will contribute to a much greater deliverance and glory for Israel. The "thoughts of the LORD" and "his plan" are key terms in the book of Isaiah and denote the paradoxical and amazing ways in which God is working out salvation for his people. God has a plan, it will prevail, it is incredible, and very profound (Pss 40:6; 92:6; Isa 5:19; 14:26; 25:1; 28:29; 46:10–11; 55:8–9). Sinners have plans too, but God will frustrate them and bring them to nothing (Ps 33:10–11; Gen 6:5; Pss 56:6; 94:11; Isa 19:3; 55:7; 59:7). Micah recognizes that his theology is hard to accept or understand, but he urges his readers to trust God and be confident about the future. God's thoughts and ways of doing things go far beyond human methods and understanding.

Micah's message brings tremendous comfort to those who are hurt, broken, and disillusioned. It is hard to comprehend all the heartache that there is in the world because of crooked politicians, greedy businessmen, and hypocritical church leaders (see for example Matt 9:36). But Micah's message to those who are suffering is that God knows and that God will come to heal, to gather, and to restore. Jesus is the Good Shepherd who calls his sheep by name, leads them out, and gathers them into one flock (John 10:1–16). Believers who have been abused and wounded by Christian leaders may take comfort that Jesus himself will heal, protect, and lead them. Wolff observed that "there is no reference to Israel, its leaders and teachers. A mission emanating from God's people is not even hinted at. The Lord himself and the Lord alone establishes something entirely new, something that appears in the midst of the world of peoples coming from the direction of Zion. He establishes new realities."[21]

---

21. Wolff, *Micah the Prophet*, 87.

Consequently, despite past disappointments, Christians can be expectant: people may often disappoint, but God will never let them down.

In light of verse 8, it is also good for pastors to note the centrality and dominion of Christ in salvation history and the biblical message. The Bible, the gospel, and God's kingdom are about Jesus; it is not about our success, our physical healing, or our financial prosperity. In fact, the early disciples of Jesus were called to leave everything and follow him. For them following Jesus meant becoming poor, loosing face, and accepting a life of servanthood. Why should it be any different for us today? If preachers have everything the world desires why should people believe them when they exhort others not to store up treasures on earth but in heaven? Rather, our lives should demonstrate that the greatest treasure is to know him and to be in his kingdom, because if we have him we have everything that we possibly could want. To be in his arms is the safest and best place to be; our eternal security and happiness are assured. Micah also teaches that God can turn apparent defeats into our greatest and most amazing victories. It seemed that Daniel was defeated by his enemies and abandoned by God when he was thrown into the lion's den, yet he not only miraculously survived but all his enemies were devoured and God's power was widely acknowledged. Paul was often hungry, homeless, weary, reviled, and persecuted; and yet, he writes, "dying, and yet we live on; beaten, and yet not killed; sorrowful, yet always rejoicing; poor, yet making many rich; having nothing, and yet possessing everything" (2 Cor 6:9–10). Indeed, for the Christian, because of what Jesus has done and is doing, suffering leads to glory. Only Christians can have this assurance and hope.

4:13–5:1 Israel as God's Instrument

Whereas before the prophet exhorted the remnant to brace themselves for more suffering, he now exhorts them to prepare for victorious action. The command "to thresh" links the section to the "threshing floor" of the previous line. Ironically, nations are coming against Israel so that God's judgment may fall upon them. In exile, the daughter of Zion will be undefeatable and will become a hammer of devastation upon all those who persecute her. But, again paradoxically, as we consider the imagery of threshing, blessing is implied for the Gentile nations. As the process of threshing extracts wheat from the chaff, so too God's judgment upon the Gentiles may result in a harvest of good grain. Even though Gentiles intended their action for evil, God turned it around for good! Therefore, the language about the ban or the devotion of their wealth to the Lord may also be understood in a positive light.

We consider that the first verse of chapter 5, like most translators and commentators, is still part of the last vision in chapter 4. It continues the thought of preparation for warfare in the face of opposition against God's people and their ruler. Many commentators proposed that the verse reflects the events surrounding Sennacherib's threat to Jerusalem in 701 BC (see 2 Kgs 18:13–19:37; 2 Chr 32:1–23; Isa 36–37). However, this explanation lacks evidence and is unnecessary. The description does not correspond well to the Rabshakeh's intimidation of Jerusalem in 701 BC. So too, Andersen notes, "There is no record of a king of Judah suffering such a fate in the time of Micah, so no identification is possible."[22] Rather, it is better to understand the text as a reference to the fall of Samaria in 722 BC, as well as a prediction of the fall of Jerusalem in 586 BC. In particular, the text refers to "a siege against us," whereas no siege was laid against Jerusalem in 701 BC.[23] In fact, in 2 Kings 19:32 the prophet Isaiah declared that Sennacherib will not "build a siege ramp" against Jerusalem (see also Isa 37:33). On the other hand, we note that a siege was laid against both Samaria and Jerusalem when the cities fell into the hands of their enemies (2 Kgs 17:5; 2 Kgs 25:1–2). The expression "they will strike Israel's ruler (i.e. judge) on the cheek with a rod" is a metaphorical reference to the humiliation that the kings of Israel and Judah endured when they were taken into captivity, but it was also a prophecy that was ultimately fulfilled in Jesus (see Matt 26:67; 27:30; Mark 14:65; 15:19; Luke 23:63–65; John 18:22; 19:1).

---

22. Andersen, *Micah: A New Translation with Introduction and Commentary*, 461.
23. Although Sennacherib boasted to have captured Hezekiah "like a bird in a cage," he never conquered Jerusalem. See James B. Pritchard, *The Ancient Near East. Volume 1: An Anthology of Texts and Pictures* (Princeton: Princeton University Press, 1973), 199–201.

CHRISTIANITY AND PEACE

The world is extraordinarily violent. Throughout history wars have devastated nations and caused unimaginable suffering. Even today, despite so many horrific lessons from the past, violence and cruelty are still devouring large chunks of humanity. The contrast between political reality for millions and the beautiful vision of peace in Micah 4:1–4 cannot be greater. What does the future hold? What are the prospects for world peace? What does the Bible say? What should be the attitude of Christians?

According to the Bible, there will indeed be global peace in the future (Zech 9:10; Rev 21–22). However, it will not be achieved through human endeavor or institutions. The solution to the scourge of war does not lie in political efforts, international organizations, or even peace treaties between nations. Rather, the root cause of hatred, violence, and war is a spiritual one – there is a fundamental problem with the human heart – and, therefore, there needs to be a spiritual solution. In short, the reason why there is no peace in the world is because of sin which produces shattered relationships. As the result of the fall, people's relationship with God, one another, the environment, and their own true selves have been broken. Instead of humility, kindness, and justice, the heart is full of pride, cruelty, and all kinds of lusts. It is only when the human being recognizes the evil of his or her attitudes and actions, receives a new heart, and experiences reconciliation with God that new relationships of healing, harmony, and peace will follow. Consequently, peace will only be achieved through God's action by means of the gospel of Jesus. It starts with spiritual regeneration of the heart when people realize their need for reconciliation with God, come to faith in Jesus, pursue lives of righteousness and mercy, and become peacemakers in their families, at work, and in their communities.

Therefore, the Christian's perspective, lifestyle, and aims must be governed by Jesus who is both Savior and Lord. Jesus' salvific work, teachings, and example inspire and guide the Christian's endeavors for peace. Jesus came to sacrifice himself as a peace offering to God, reconciling humanity to God and uniting Jew and Gentile into one family. He instructed his disciples to be disseminators of peace (see Matt 5:9; 10:13; Mark 9:50) and consistently denounced the use of aggression in his teachings (Matt 5:38–48; 26:51–52). It is not surprising, therefore, that many early Christian writers were pacifists. However, with the conversion of Constantine, Christianity became intertwined with politics and the ideas of pacifism did not gain much traction in the political establishment and remained on the edges of society. As a result, Christianity did not save Europe from war; the era of Christendom was as bloody as any other in the history of the world.

Nevertheless, Christianity, when the teachings and example of Jesus came to the fore, has had a very positive impact upon civilization. Since the

Bible teaches that humanity was created in the image of God, Christianity places huge value on human life. It was largely through the dissemination of Christian values in the Roman Empire that abortion, infanticide, gladiatorial contests, slavery, prostitution, and pederasty were outlawed in civil society. In addition, the Christian emphasis on love, inspired acts of compassion, mercy, and philanthropy. Convictions about "inalienable human rights" – such as life, liberty, and the pursuit of happiness – have been shaped primarily within a Christian context.

> *Lord, make me an instrument of your peace.*
> *Where there is hatred, let me sow love;*
> *Where there is injury, pardon;*
> *Where there is doubt, faith;*
> *Where there is despair, hope;*
> *Where there is darkness, light;*
> *Where there is sadness, joy.*
>
> (Saint Francis of Assisi)

On a practical level, Christians should be peacemakers in the following ways. Firstly, they need to grasp God's concern for peace and earnestly pray for peace. Secondly, they need to emulate the humility and kindness of Jesus in their daily lives. Christians need to stop fighting among themselves, maintain unity, and let the gospel transform their hearts. At work or at home they must stop lashing out, cease from slandering others, and refrain from using harsh words (Ps 34:14; 1 Cor 7:17; 1 Thess 5:13). Then, thirdly, they should be peacemakers in their families, in marriage, in church, and in society, living peaceful and quiet lives (Phil 4:4–9). But, ultimately, perfect peace will only come when Jesus returns to destroy the enemies of peace and complete his reign.

MICAH 5

Chapter 5 is closely related to the themes of the preceding chapter and continues Micah's Message of Restoration. It focuses on the coming deliverer through whom God will restore his people and establish his universal kingdom of peace. It contains one of the most remarkable messianic prophecies in the Bible which was fulfilled in Jesus.

5:2–5a The Ruler from Bethlehem

The next section about the royal ruler who is to come from Bethlehem is one of the great messianic prophecies in the Old Testament. It is a carefully drafted oracle and placed strategically in the middle section of Micah, being central to the Message of Restoration. After the visions of universal peace and divine rule (Mic 4:1–8), this oracle explains more clearly how God is going to bring about the new era of peace. He is going to raise up a ruler from Bethlehem – from the line of David – whose kingdom will powerfully extend to the ends of the earth. Similarly, Wolff states that Micah 4:8–5:4 tells us how the royal rule will take place.[24] Many keywords in the passage link the oracle with the preceding narrative, indicating that the prophet is providing a sequence of sketches how the future restoration will take place (see Figure 14).

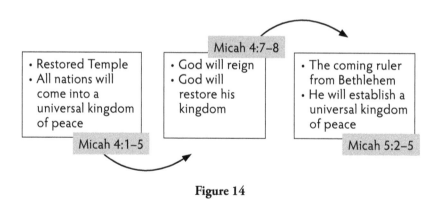

Figure 14

In verse 2 the first word in Hebrew, translated "but you," provides both a link and a contrast with the previous verse. In Hebrew, the adverb "now" in verse 1 (*'atah*) and the pronoun "you" (*'atah*) in verse 2 sound exactly the same and thus affords a smooth literary transition from the theme of defeat to the theme of victory, implying that these disparate historical experiences

---

24. Wolff, *Micah the Prophet*, 90.

form part of an integrated whole. In the previous verse the ruler or judge of Israel (i.e. the king) will be opposed and rejected in apparent defeat, however in the subsequent section Israel's future ruler will be victorious. In the Old Testament, in marked contrast with Samaria and Jerusalem, Bethlehem is not a significant town and neither does it have any strategic importance. In the text "small" indicates its low status. However, Micah already noted that God's ways are different from human ways, and that he uses the humble to confound the proud, bringing victory out of apparent defeat (Mic 4:11–12). The key idea of verse 2 is that even though Bethlehem is not a very significant town, yet a mighty ruler will come from it. Hillers insightfully observed that the promise of the coming ruler implies a criticism of the current king.[25] "Ephrathah" is an ancient name of the region of Bethlehem (see Gen 35:16, 19; 48:7; 1 Sam 17:12). Whereas Bethlehem means "house of bread," Ephrathah means "fruitful." According to Limburg, this double identification of Bethlehem was added to distinguish it from the town called Bethlehem in Zebulon (see Josh 19:15).[26] Although Bethlehem is insignificant from a political, economic, and military perspective, Israel's most beloved King David came from this rural settlement (see Figure 15). The original readers of Micah would have been very familiar with this history and would therefore naturally associate the future ruler with the house of David. In the Davidic covenant, God promised that there would always be a Davidic king on the throne of Israel (2 Sam 7:8–16; compare Ps 89). This tradition is expanded in Isaiah in conjunction with a future kingdom of global peace (Isa 9:6–7, 11). Furthermore, the overlapping themes and shared terminology in many Old Testament passages about the coming deliverer, the Davidic ruler, the Messiah, and a new era of prosperity and peace imply that these ideas are closely related and describe the same future eschatological event (see Gen 49:8–12; Ps 72; Isa 61:1–3; 66:18–21; Dan 7:13–14; 9:24–27). Therefore, traditional Christian interpretation has regarded such passages as "messianic" and has seen their fulfillment in the coming of the Lord Jesus and the kingdom of God.

---

25. Hillers, *Micah: A Commentary on the Book of the Prophet Micah*, 66.
26. Limburg, *Hosea-Micah. Interpretation: A Bible Commentary for Teaching and Preaching*, 186.

Micah 4-5: The Message of Restoration

Figure 15. Modern Bethlehem

More astonishingly, after the disclosure of the Davidic roots of the coming ruler, the vision boldly identifies his divine nature. The phrase "for me" stands at the beginning of the sentence and emphasizes that the ruler will be God's agent and will come to fulfill God's intentions. But, moreover, the term "ruler" links the prophecy with Micah 4:7-8, thereby connecting the reign of this coming ruler with the prophecy of the Lord's reign over Mount Zion. The term is used elsewhere to describe the Davidic ruler (2 Sam 23:3; 2 Chr 7:18), but very significantly it more frequently describes God's rule (2 Chr 20:6; Pss 22:28; 66:7; 89:10; 103:19; Isa 40:10). Therefore, again, as in Micah 2:13, this future ruler will not just be a Davidic descendant, but the Lord himself. In order to remove all doubt as to the identity of the coming ruler, Micah unambiguously confirms his divine attributes with the last phrase of verse 2, his origin is "from ancient times, from the days of eternity." Although translators and some commentaries have tempered the words to, "whose origins are from of old, from ancient times" (NIV), there is little doubt that the traditional rendering is to be preferred.[27] The Hebrew term *'olam* used here may indicate "ancient times," "antiquity," or a "long time," but it also

---

27. See Waltke, *Micah: An Introduction and Commentary*, 183. The ESV has, "whose coming forth is from of old, from ancient days;" the NET has, "one whose origins are in the distant past;" the NLT has, "one whose origins are from the distant past;" the NRSV has, "whose origin is from of old, from ancient days." On the other hand the KJV has, "whose goings forth *have*

regularly has the meaning of "all time" or "eternity" (Gen 9:16; 17:7; 21:33; Pss 25:6; 90:2; 103:17; 145:13; Isa 45:17; Jer 10:10; Ezek 16:60; 37:26). The translation "from ancient times" is meaningless unless we are to believe in the existence of supercentenarians. The eternity of the coming ruler is already intimated in passages such as Isaiah 9:6–7. In the Message of Restoration where the term is used, its meaning is also clearly "everlasting" (Mic 4:5, 7).[28] These messianic prophecies and expectations are perfectly fulfilled in the person of Jesus according to the New Testament writers.

According to the context, verse 3 states that even though "Israel will be abandoned" and will go into exile, it will only be for a limited period until the arrival of the promised ruler. The birth imagery is taken up again (see Micah 4:9–10) to describe the suffering that Israel will experience before the arrival of the new ruler. In the Old Testament Israel is frequently personified as a woman (e.g. Hos 1–2; *Song of Songs*). The promise to Eve about the seed who will destroy the works of the devil will be fulfilled (Gen 3:15); the Savior of the world will come from Israel. Birth is a painful process, but it produces new life. So too, the book of Isaiah asserts that the suffering of Israel lays the foundation for the restoration that is to follow, it even has a vicarious element associated with it. After the "labor" there will be restoration; the people of Israel will return and be restored together. There are a number of ways to interpret the expression "the rest of his brothers." The "rest" may refer to those who are left over after war or who have survived a struggle, or it may refer to those who have been rejected or despised by others. Either interpretation makes sense within the context. They will return to the children of Israel or they will return with the children of Israel. As David united the twelve tribes, and even drew Gentiles into his kingdom as well, so too the coming ruler will unite all God's people together – Jew and Gentile will come together as one in God's new remnant (see Mic 4:6–7).

Verse 4 continues to describe the activity of the promised ruler. He will stand firmly and will shepherd his people. Whereas the previous verse took up the imagery of a woman in child birth, this verse recalls the imagery of God as the shepherd of his people (see Mic 12:12–13; 4:8; compare Ps 23; Ezek 36). His reign will be security and peace, and it will extend even to the ends of the earth. Again, we note that the passages portraying future restoration refer to

---

been from of old, from everlasting." So too, the NASB has, "His goings forth are from long ago, From the days of eternity." The Septuagint translated the phrase as, "whose origins are from the beginning, from the days of eternity."

28. In Micah 7:14 the term is used in the sense of "ancient times."

Micah 4-5: The Message of Restoration

the same complex of events. Even though this future restoration is described in different sections of the book of Micah and from a variety of angles, it relates to the same era. With each additional description, more precise information is given on how the restoration will come about. In chapter 2:12–13 God will gather his scattered flock, in chapter 4:1–4 Jerusalem will become the most prominent place of learning for the nations, and now in chapter 5:1–6 we note that it will be accomplished through the coming of a new ruler.

The main exegetical question that this prophecy raises concerns the identity of this coming ruler. A careful analysis of the passage will provide a persuasive answer. The passage makes at least eight assertions about the coming ruler: (1) he will be from Bethlehem; (2) he will be a ruler (probably from the lineage of David); (3) he will gather or unite the people of God; (4) he will stand firm amidst opposition; (5) he will shepherd the flock of God; (6) he will provide security and peace; (7) his influence will extend over the whole world; (8) and, finally, he will be the Lord himself. After the New Testament era and 2,000 years of Christian history, the obvious and only name that comes up in everyone's mind is that of Jesus. Already in the first century AD, the author of the Gospel of Matthew quoted Micah 5:2 as having been fulfilled in Jesus (Matt 2:6). Although some objectors contend that Jesus did not fulfill some criteria identified in this prophecy, we may well maintain, based on a biblical understanding of how prophetic literature works, that the New Testament writers correctly identified the promised ruler with Jesus.

A whole book can be written to show how Jesus fulfilled each of the criteria identified above. Here we will just make the following comments, addressing the eight criteria identified above. (1) Based on historical investigation Jesus was born in Bethlehem. (2) Although Jesus was not a "political" king, many ascribed the title to him and obeyed him as a king. We have noticed the spiritual nature of his kingdom in Micah's prophecies; people would come to learn God's law and God would be their teacher. Jesus was also from the line of David. (3) Jesus is uniting all of God's people from every race together (Jews and Gentiles). This is one of the greatest emphases of the New Testament (see Acts 10:34, 47; Gal 3:28; Eph 2:11–16; Col 1:17–20). (4) Jesus was opposed by many Jews and Gentiles during his life on earth, yet persisted in his conviction about the kingdom of God and in his role to be the suffering servant. Throughout history many have continued to oppose and persecute Christians. (5) Jesus performed the function of a shepherd in leading and caring for those who followed him. One of the main images of Jesus in the New Testament is that of the shepherd (Mark 14:27; John 10:7–18; Heb 13:20; 1 Pet 2:25).

(6) Jesus rejected violence and war, and had been an influence for peace in the world (Matt 5:38–42; 26:52; 27:11–14; Luke 22:49–51). (7) Of course, many historians observed that Jesus has been the most influential person in history. There is probably not a nation today without Christians and there is hardly any area of human endeavor that has not been influenced by Christianity. (8) Finally, we may also note, in line with orthodox Christianity, that Jesus is more than a human person and a descendant of David, but is also confessed to be the Son of God. As we have argued, the text identifies the coming ruler with the Lord. In the book of Micah and the rest of Scripture, the Lord is the pre-eminent ruler and shepherd of his people. This central belief links the activity of the coming ruler with the Lord's role as ruler and shepherd. Furthermore, the phrase "from the days of eternity" (v. 2) clearly indicates that the coming ruler is more than human. In the Bible only two forms of intelligent life are known apart from human beings – angels and God (the devil and evil spirits are fallen angels). In other words, if the promised ruler is more than a human being, he is either an angel or God himself. In the rest of Scripture there is no indication that the future deliverer of Israel will be an angel. Instead, God is frequently described as the deliverer or savior of Israel. Therefore, the conclusion is that the coming ruler will be none other than Yahweh himself. In fact, many other passages in the Old Testament make this identification (see Isa 9:6–11; 40:9–11). Noticeably, the ascription of divinity to the person of Jesus has deep biblical roots and was not an idea invented by the early church.

In conclusion, we may also observe that there is no uncertainty regarding the genuineness of this prediction about the coming ruler. Some doubt that the prophecies concerning the fall of Samaria and the fall of Jerusalem were genuine prophecies written before these events. However, when it comes to the greater prophecies about the coming ruler – that the Messiah will be born in Bethlehem and that his kingdom will have global influence – all reasonable skepticism is removed. As the Belgic Confession states, "even the blind can see" that these prophecies are being fulfilled.

BETHLEHEM AS THE BIRTHPLACE OF JESUS

We would like to take this opportunity to address the recent contention by some Jesus Research scholars that the tradition of Jesus' birth in Bethlehem does not bear historical scrutiny. Rather, some argue that Jesus was born in Nazareth and that Matthew made up the story about the birth in Bethlehem to show that Jesus was fulfilling Old Testament prophecy. After all, they argue, Jesus was known as "Jesus of Nazareth," not as "Jesus of Bethlehem." Most current scholars examining the life of Jesus, although they do not regard all the information in the Gospels as reliable, still consider that the Gospels contain much historical information about Jesus. Indeed, because of new archaeological findings and documentary research, there has been a dramatic shift in perspective regarding the historical reliability of the Gospels over the last thirty years.

According to James H. Charlesworth, a leading figure in Jesus Research, scholars may use the following five criteria to assess the historical reliability of traditions in the Gospels regarding Jesus: (1) embarrassment; (2) dissimilarity; (3) multiple attestation; (4) coherence; (5) Palestinian Jewish setting. He goes on to list "ten additional supporting methods," which are also perceptive, but we will focus on the five main ones in this discussion.[1] We will argue that on the basis of at least four of these criteria that the tradition of Jesus' birth in Bethlehem is historically accurate.

Firstly, the strongest evidence for the birth of Jesus in Bethlehem is the multiple attestations of sources. Three Gospels attest to this tradition (Matthew, Luke, and John) and what is particularly persuasive is that their traditions about the birth in Bethlehem are independent from Mark and from one another. Scholars attributed the Bethlehem story in Matthew to a source labeled "M" (Matt 2:1–18) and the story in Luke to a source labeled "L" (Luke 2:1–20). The abbreviations M and L indicate sources or material that are unique to the respective Gospels. The disparities between Matthew's account and Luke's account of Jesus' birth show that at a very early date (c. 40–60 AD) different traditions about Jesus' birth were circulating within the circles of the Palestinian Jesus Movement. There are major differences in the details of the two birth narratives, yet the common factor is the location at Bethlehem. In addition to Matthew and Luke, the Gospel of John is also certainly aware about the tradition that Jesus was born in Bethlehem, which is expressed with the Gospel's characteristic use of irony (John 7:40–43). In addition to these first century sources, early church tradition unanimously places the birth in Bethlehem (e.g. Justin Martyr, Irenaeus, Tertullian, Hippolytus, Origen, Jerome, Eusebius). No one in the early church identified Nazareth as the location of Jesus' birth. Moreover, the construction of a pre-Byzantine chapel in Bethlehem to mark the place of the birth corroborates this belief (see Figure 16).[2] On the other hand, there is no church in Nazareth that was built to mark the place of Jesus' birth.

Figure 16: The Church of the nativity in Bethlehem (Berthold Werner/Wikimedia Commons)[3]

Secondly, the criteria of dissimilarity may also be used to argue for the Bethlehem birth. As many Jesus Research scholars have pointed out, Jesus is regularly identified as being from Nazareth and not from Bethlehem. Placing the birth at Bethlehem, therefore, creates a difficulty for the early propagators of the Jesus tradition. If everyone knew Jesus as the one "from Nazareth," the Bethlehem story would be inconsistent with this tradition. If the early evangelists could fabricate stories, it would have been much easier and natural to locate Jesus' birth in Nazareth. In other words, there must have been important reasons why all the Gospel writers who referred to Jesus' birth placed the location in Bethlehem. The argument that Matthew simply used the prophecy from Micah 5:2 as the basis of his story in order to prove that Jesus fulfilled prophecy is not very convincing. Any number of places in Old Testament passages could have been used for the location of Jesus' birth to create the impression that Jesus fulfilled prophecy. For example, Matthew may have placed the birth in Nazareth and quoted from Isaiah 9:1–7 to show that Israel's deliverer is to come from the region of Galilee. Alternative, he may have placed the birth in Egypt and quoted the passage from Hosea 11:1. Rather, it is more probable that Matthew recalled Micah 5:2 because he knew about the Bethlehem tradition from Jesus' early followers and family.

Figure 17. The star indicates the place, according to tradition, where Jesus was born under the Church of the Nativity in Bethlehem

Thirdly, in terms of the criteria of coherence, Jesus' followers regarded him as being a descendant of David. It is not known how genealogies were kept in the first century, but such records or traditions clearly existed as a number of families had genealogical knowledge of their ancestry. The Gospel writers traced both Joseph and Mary's genealogies back to King David, and Bethlehem, being the city of David, coheres with this tradition. And, fourthly, the Bethlehem tradition also accords with the Palestinian Jewish setting of Jesus' ministry and teachings. Even though Jesus' family settled in Nazareth, the family's origin stems from Judea. It was only after the Maccabean revolt that Galilee was resettled by Jews from Judea. These Jews would have been very patriotic (like the Jewish settlers in the West Bank today) as they saw themselves as the legitimate inheritors of the Promised Land. We learn from the Gospels and early church tradition that many of Jesus' extended family still lived around Jerusalem in the first century AD (e.g. the family of John the Baptist). This wider Judean Jewish context of Jesus' family coheres with the place of his birth in Bethlehem, which is just a few kilometers south of Jerusalem. Therefore, there is sound historical evidence to support the tradition that Jesus was born in Bethlehem. Based on all the sources and the criteria of Jesus Research methodology, it is more probable that Jesus was born in Bethlehem than in Nazareth.

---

1. See James H. Charlesworth, *An Essential Guide: The Historical Jesus* (Nashville: Abingdon Press, 2008).
2. This church is the oldest church building that survived the turbulent history of Israel.
3. Image: Bethlehem Church of the Nativity by Berthold Werner via https://commons.wikimedia.org/wiki/File:Bethlehem_BW_10.JPG.

Micah

Fulfilled Prophecy

The biggest point of application from this prophecy about the coming ruler from Bethlehem is that the gospel is true and that one should believe that Jesus is Savior and Lord (Luke 2:11). The prophet Micah predicted sometime in the eighth century BC that a king would come from Bethlehem and that he would be great to the ends of the earth. This prophecy has been spectacularly fulfilled with the birth of Jesus in Bethlehem and the spread of Christianity across the world. Millions throughout history have confessed Jesus to be their shepherd king and have found joy and peace. These three things are all undeniable facts, viz. (1) Micah in the eighth century BC predicted that a ruler would come from Bethlehem; (2) Jesus was born in the little town of Bethlehem; and (3) millions of people from around the world have claimed Jesus to be their King, Lord, and Savior. One of the main purposes of predictive prophecy in the Bible is to show that the fulfillment of the event prophesied is due to God's action. Therefore, one may be assured that Jesus' birth in Bethlehem was not an ordinary event.

Faith involves at least two aspects: firstly, there must be knowledge based on rational analysis of evidence, but then, secondly, there must also be personal commitment and action based on that knowledge. That Jesus came fulfilling many biblical prophecies is one of the key evidences of the truth of the gospel. But knowing these facts is not enough; they need to lead to personal assent, trust, and confession that Jesus is Savior and Lord. Believers, who have acknowledged Jesus as the Savior, must also follow him as Lord of their lives. They must become good citizens of his kingdom, be gentle, and become instruments of his peace in their families, in their work place, and in their societies.

Considering the fulfillment of this prophecy in the little town of Bethlehem also reminds us of "the secret of the kingdom" (Mark 4:11), that in the kingdom of God small beginnings may have great endings and that seemingly unimportant incidents may have great significance (Mark 4:26–32). Who would have thought that the rural village of Bethlehem would become one of the most famous places in the world? Who would have thought that the homeless young woman would give birth to the Savior of the world? Who would have thought that Jesus' death on the cross would have precipitated the greatest movement the world has ever seen? God's plans and ways of doing things are certainly very different from ours, as Paul also reminds us, "the foolishness of God is wiser than human wisdom, and the weakness of God is stronger than human strength" (1 Cor 1:25). In other words, Christian workers across Asia, irrespective of their circumstances, should not lose heart, but may be very confident about the results of their ministry.

5:5b–6 Interlude Regarding Ongoing Struggle and Victory

There has been a wide range of opinion regarding the meaning of these few lines. Some regard it as a failed, and hence, genuine prophecy. Others suggest that these words may have been the message of the false prophets who prophesied that Israel would be able to resist any attack by Assyria or Babylon. Others see it as a reference to Cyrus, under whose rule many Jews were able to return to the land. Still, other interpreters relate the prophecy to the eschatological future and propose that the prophecy awaits fulfillment. We suggest, according to the context and in line with the overall framework of salvation history, that the prophecy refers to the time after the coming of the ruler mentioned in verse 2 (i.e. to the New Testament or church era). Like the epilogue to the vision in Micah 4:1–5, it provides a corrective to unbounded optimism. Even though the Messiah will set up a new kingdom that will be spectacularly successful, there will still be struggle and opposition. The term "Assyrian," therefore, refers symbolically to those who oppose God's kingdom and the gospel. "Nimrod" was the tyrannical ancestor of both the Assyrians and the Babylonians and it is possible that the name is based on the verbal root meaning "rebellion" (see Gen 10:8–12; 1 Chr 1:10). According to Calvin, the description of Nimrod as a "mighty hunter before the Lord" indicates that Nimrod tried to claim special status for himself.[29] We understand "seven shepherds, even eight commanders" to mean that God will raise up many able leaders throughout history to protect the church against all kinds of challenges. So too, Smith comments, "The seven shepherds and eight leaders are not to be taken literally. This is a Hebrew literary device to indicate that an indefinite yet adequate number of leaders will arise to overthrow the Assyrians (Prov 30:15, 18, 21, 29; Eccl 11:2)."[30] Therefore, we again disagree with Alfaro who sees a contradiction between verse 4 and verse 6.[31] Rather, as in chapter 4:5, this new reign will not immediately extinguish all opposition, the enemy of God's people will still be able to launch incursions. However, the difference now is that the church will be able to withstand the attacks, and will also carry out the role of shepherd in

---

29. There are interesting similarities between the biblical Nimrod and the Mesopotamian legendary king Gilgamesh.
30. Ralph L. Smith, *Micah-Malachi*, 45.
31. Alfaro, *Justice and Loyalty: A Commentary on the Book of Micah*, 43.

the lands of hostility. "He will deliver us" refers to Christ's ongoing protection of his people until complete victory at the end of the age.

5:7–9 The Role of the Remnant

The following section describes the role of God's people being light to the nations while they are exiled in foreign lands. In the first instance, it refers to the Babylonian exile, but more particularly the prophecy relates to the time after the coming of the promised ruler in verse 2 (i.e. the era of the New Testament). According to verse 7, the "remnant" will be a blessing, and according to verse 8, they will be invincible. Several New Testament writers applied the theme of exile to the Gentile church (see Heb 11:13; Jas 1:1; 1 Pet 1:1–2; 2:11) in order to describe the church's current position in the world. In this picture of exile, the people of God will not be gathered together in one place where the nations will come to receive blessing; instead, they will be scattered throughout the world to be a blessing. "Dew" is a positive symbol and refers to divine blessing (Gen 27:28; Deut 33:13, 28; Ps 133:3; Prov 19:12; Isa 26:19; Hos 14:6; Zech 8:12). In Deuteronomy 32:2 dew is also used as a symbol for God's word. According to Wolff, dew is "unobtrusive, hardly noticed, and yet extremely effective."[32] Alfaro's observation is also perceptive, "The promises made to David were to be fulfilled in the same manner as the promises made to Abraham, through gradual and silent unfolding throughout history."[33]

Likewise, the expression "like showers on the grass" (or "abundant rains") indicates divine blessing (Pss 65:11; 72:6) and is also used in Deuteronomy 32:2 as a symbol for God's teaching. This promise that God's people will be like the blessing of dew among the nations also occurs in the eighth century prophet Hosea (Hos 13:3; 14:6). But, the remnant will not only bring blessing, they will also bring consternation and even destruction to the nations. The picture of future blessing is again balanced with the element of opposition and conflict. Biblical eschatology does not only present a picture of future utopian bliss; it carefully balances anticipation of blessing and bliss with struggle and suffering. Therefore, the New Testament experience of both blessing and persecution, both victory and defeat, and both joy and sorrow has a thorough Old Testament background (see 2 Cor 6:1–10). These contrasting images of God's people as both blessing and curse reflect the promises of the Abrahamic covenant, many will be blessed but those who oppose Abraham will be condemned (Gen 12:2–3).

---

32. Wolff, *Micah the Prophet*, 95.
33. Alfaro, *Justice and Loyalty: A Commentary on the Book of Micah*, 58.

CHRISTIAN REVIVAL AND CHURCH RENEWAL

In this passage, there is a beautiful image of how God's people even in exile – or precisely because of the exile – will be a blessing to the world. Micah uses three similes to describe the church in the world: dew, rain, and a lion. Dew is essential for nourishment of dry areas, especially arid regions like Israel. Without dew much vegetation supporting livestock will dry up and wither. And, yet, dew is quiet and unpretentious in operation. God's people today function in the same way. According to Jesus, they are the salt and light of the world (Matt 5:13–14). Society or life without the influence of Christians will be very gloomy and crude. When we look at the contribution of Christianity to civilization over the last two thousand years, we note that this is indeed the case. Medicine, universal education, science and technology, human rights, kindness and compassion are largely due to the influence of Christians in the world.[1] Churches or Christians should not be discouraged because they are not many. The influence of Christians goes far beyond their number in society. In fact, true Christians have always been a minority. Yet, the blessing that true Christians bring for families, in workplaces, and in societies cannot be over estimated. Christians are gentle, kind, honest, helpful, and through their prayers bring uncountable benefits to those around them. Undoubtedly, they are the best friends, the best employees, and the best citizens.

The third metaphor that Micah uses is also very informative: Christians are lions. The lion is the king of the animal world and those who challenge it come off second best. Of course, this image relates to spiritual warfare and does not mean that Christians should physically attack their enemies. Rather, Christians use truth, the word of God, and love to overcome opposition and break down strongholds (see Rom 12:14–20; Eph 6:10–20). Jesus is not a political king and his "kingdom is not of this world" (John 18:36). Unfortunately, in history many Christians did not understand this central truth and have taken up the sword against their enemies. For example, in China Hong Xiuquan wanted to throw off the Manchu rulers and establish his own Taiping Heavenly Kingdom through the use of force. He raised an army of one million and created untold suffering and havoc throughout China. This is just the opposite of Jesus' example and teaching. Jesus never took up the sword; in fact, he counseled just the opposite, "all who draw the sword will die by the sword" (Matt 26:52), and "if anyone slaps you on the right cheek, turn to them the other cheek also" (Matt 5:39), and "love your enemies" (Matt 5:44). If Christians had taken these words to heart, in many instances history would have been very different. According to Wolff, "When the founder of peace from Zion is unrecognized and despised, then the wrath of God is at work in tumultuous turbulences."[2]

---

1. For example, see Alvin J. Schmidt, *How Christianity Changed the World* (Grand Rapids, Michigan: Zondervan, 2001). According to R. R. Palmer, "It is impossible to exaggerate the importance of the coming of Christianity." *A History of the Modern World.* 10th edition (McGraw-Hill, 2007/ New York: Knopf, 4th edition, 1971), 16. Also note, Vishal Mangalwadi, *The Book that Made your World: How the Bible Created the Soul of Western Civilization* (Nashville, Tennessee: Thomas Nelson), 2011.
2. Wolff, *Micah the Prophet*, 98.

5:10–15 The Destruction of Idolatry

In line with the previous visions in the book of Micah, which address Israel and Judah, the pronouns – "your houses," "your chariots," "your land," "your strongholds," "your witchcraft," and "your idols" – refer to God's people. Therefore, this startling prophecy announces that God has had enough of Israel's idolatry. He will not only cut off all the ungodly (5:9), but will also come to cut off all the idolatry of his people. It seems that judgment not only begins with the house of God, it also ends with the house of God. The expression "in that day" locates the fulfillment of this prophecy to the same general era that has been outlined in the previous visions. Of course, it does not refer to one specific time, but anticipate a process of time in which the destruction of idolatry will transpire. The verb "to destroy" or "to cut off" (*karath*) occurs four times in this passage. In addition to its basic meaning "to cut off," it also means "to root out" or "to eliminate." However, the most important theological use of the verb is "to cut" a covenant, referring to the "cutting" or offering of a sacrifice at the establishment of a covenant. Old Testament covenants, like most covenants in the Ancient Near East, involved rewards for obedience as well as punishments for disobedience. In other words, covenant disobedience will attract severe punishment. So too, since God is faithful, he will not stand idly by when his covenant is transgressed by his people. But, paradoxically, God's punishment of Israel will mean their salvation, since the punishment removes the things which cause his people to sin. God will destroy the military infrastructure (i.e. the things on which his people depend for security); their strong cities (i.e. the things in which his people take pride); as well as all their idols (i.e. the things for which they crave). The last verse is a summary statement, which refers not just to Israel, but to all nations. Gentile nations who saw the witness of God's scattered remnant and heard the truth of God's word must respond appropriately. Biblical revelation portrays God as one who cannot tolerate any form of idolatry and as one who will come to judge humanity. The command "to hear" or "to obey" occurs six times in the book of Micah (Mic 1:2; 3:1, 9; 6:1, 2, 9). This stark warning prepares the reader for the next section in the book, the Message of Reconciliation.

Eradicating Idolatry

In response to this prophecy about God's coming judgment upon idolatry, Christians and the church must remove all idols from their midst and from their hearts. We should not think that because we have no statues of Buddha or Vishnu in our churches and homes that we are without idols. Our idols may well be our 60-inch plasma TV, our luxurious home, our latest model car, or our educational degrees on the wall. Or, our idol may be the desire to become rich, to become well-known or popular, or to advance our brand. It may be the more "spiritual" idols such as our mega-church, our state-of-the-art musical performances, or our connections with the rich and powerful. In fact, our idol can even be a theological hobby horse, like some new age doctrine, *feng shui* (geomancy), the so-called "fourth dimension," teachings or emphases that are not found in God's word. We should not think that only the ancient Israelites had a problem with idolatry.

God will uproot our sacred poles from our midst. In many places judgment has already begun. In fact, it is interesting to note that before the exile Israelite society was filled with idolatry and pluralism, but after the suffering of the exile the Israelites became strictly monotheistic. The church in China underwent a similar process of purification during the Cultural Revolution (1966–1976). Mao Zedong's policy of authoritarian atheism removed much idolatry and traditional forms of superstition from Chinese society, resulting in a much purer church. On the other hand, the church in Taiwan, which did not undergo the baptism of fire of the Cultural Revolution, is often infected with the beliefs and practices of traditional Chinese folk religions, animistic practices, and *feng shui* superstitions.

MICAH 6–7:
THE MESSAGE OF RECONCILIATION

MICAH 6

After the exhilarating presentation of a glorious future of restoration and universal peace, Micah comes to the main purpose of his ministry and prophecy – the Message of Reconciliation. Despite their sins and miserable condition, God has a tremendous plan for his people in which they have an important role to play. However, before restoration will take place, there need to be thorough repentance and a change in heart. Therefore, in chapters 6 and 7, the last section of the book, there is an urgent appeal to repent and to be reconciled to God. Whereas the first section of the book deals mostly with past sin, and the second section generally with future restoration, the final section focuses on the need for reconciliation in the present. In order to bridge the gap or effect the transition between past sin and future restoration, to avoid judgment and enter into salvation, there needs to be urgent action in the form of repentance and right living in the present.

Commentators have divided the last two chapters in different ways. In chapter 6 we will follow the section division of the Masoretic scribes by dividing the chapter into two halves from verses 1 to 8 and then from verses 9 to 16. The first half of the chapter is a trial scene in which God reviews the actions of the covenant parties and presents a verdict. In the second half of the chapter, God announces judgment on all wickedness and injustice. It is much more difficult to divide chapter 7 into distinct sections with independent themes. The diversity of material, changing moods, and intermingling of themes reveal a complex compositional history with the result that it is not always easy to determine where one section concludes and the next begins.

Some commentators have proposed that the material in these chapters come from a "different hand" in the north,[1] and others have dated it to an exilic or post-exilic period (Stade and Wellhausen). However, their arguments are not convincing, are often simplistic, and always lack satisfactory evidence. The interpretation of data and construction of arguments depend solely on the subjective predispositions of the commentators. Material is interpreted

---

1. For example, see Alfaro, *Justice and Loyalty: A Commentary on the Book of Micah*, 62–63.

to accord with the writer's presuppositions about the origins of the book of Micah and contrary evidence is simply ignored. On the other hand, there are good arguments for regarding the material as pre-exilic and also stemming from the prophet Micah.

For example, A. S. van der Woude adduced five reasons to argue that chapters 6 and 7 were written by a different prophet in the north.[2] Firstly, van der Woude proposed that the first five chapters are influenced by Isaiah, whereas the last two chapters are influenced by Hosea. However, one may equally argue that the exodus motifs in the last two chapters also stem from Isaiah (see Mic 6:4–5; 7:15–16) and that material in the first part of Micah, like judgment upon Samaria and Davidic traditions, reflect influence from Hosea (see Hos 3:4–5; 7:1; 8:5–6; 10:5; 13:6). Secondly, according to van der Woude, chapters 6 and 7 never refer to places in the south but only to places in the north. If one considers the possibility that Micah prophesied during the eighth century before the fall of Samaria and addressed the northern kingdom, as the book depicts (see Mic 1:1), there is no inconsistency or problem with the presence of geographic names from the northern kingdom. And, since we have shown that a biblical prophecy may have a number of meanings and multiple fulfillments, these prophecies may also equally apply to the south. Thirdly, van der Woude argued that chapters 1 to 5 center on Zion traditions, whereas chapters 6 and 7 center on the northern traditions of the exodus and conquest. However, we do not accept that the traditions of the exodus and conquest belonged exclusively to the northern kingdom as Isaiah 40-50 clearly shows. Nevertheless, we already noted that exodus and conquest traditions feature prominently in Micah 2:12–13 and that Zion traditions also occur in the last two chapters of Micah (see Mic 6:6–7; 7:11–12). Fourthly, van der Woude contended that whereas chapters 1 to 5 speak to different leaders in society, the last two chapters address the people as a whole. However, this reasoning does not necessarily indicate that the two sections have a different author. The observation that the target audience is different, if correct, simply implies that the author addressed all sections of society. In fact, according to Micah 1:2, the book addresses the people of God as a whole, hence there is no inconsistency between chapters 1 to 5 and chapters 6 to 7 having a different target audience. Finally, according to van der Woude, Micah 1:1 addresses both Samaria and Jerusalem, i.e. the north and the south. This observation is

---

2. See Alfaro, *Justice and Loyalty: A Commentary on the Book of Micah*, 62. A. S. van der Woude's position was first articulated by Heinrich Ewald, *Die Propheten des Alten Bundes*, Vol. 1 (Gottingen: Vandenhoeck & Ruprecht, 1867).

obviously correct, but it does not imply that there are two different prophets or authors behind the material. In fact, it suggests the opposite, that there was one prophet addressing both the northern and southern kingdoms. We have briefly reviewed van der Woude's arguments to demonstrate that so-called "scholarly" views regarding the sources or compositional history of the book of Micah are often not much more than just subjective speculation.[3]

6:1–8 God's Dispute with His People

With a series of commands, the prophet impresses on his hearers the urgency of their current situation. The command "listen" or "obey" links the new section with the last word of Micah 5:15, which is the same word in Hebrew (*shama*). God will judge all nations who do not obey, but now the problem is with Israel who must hear and obey. With the use of keywords throughout the text, we note that the book of Micah has been carefully edited to make sense as a whole. The main burden of the prophet is that God's people should hear and obey his message. Micah is looking for a behavioral response in the lives of God's people.

In verse 1 the verb "to plead a case" (Hebrew: *rîb*) relates to legal proceedings and indicates that a contract has been breached (see Exod 23:2, 3, 6; Deut 25:1; 2 Sam 15:2, 4; Prov 25:8). The root also occurs in verse 2 as a noun and has been translated as "indictment," "controversy," "accusation," and "complaint," which implies that there was not only a legal agreement (relationship) between the Lord and his people, but also that the people breached the terms of the agreement. The language recalls the responsibilities that the Mosaic covenant placed upon Israel, which the people agreed to do (see Exod 19:7–9; Deut 5:27–29). The Lord is indicting Israel because they have violated their covenant relationship and responsibilities. Other contemporary prophets brought the same accusation against Israel and Judah (see Isa 3:13; 57:16; Hos 4:1; 12:3). Evidently, the Lord's main argument or problem is not with the pagan nations, but with his own people.

The keyword *rîb* also identifies this section (vv. 1–8) as belonging to the *rîb* or prophetic lawsuit genre, which intermittently occurs in prophetic literature (see Hos 4:1; 12:2; Amos 3:1–8; Jer 25:31).[4] The disputation usually

---

3. Brevard S. Childs likewise observed, "Although these scholars all agree on a complex history of redaction which passed through many stages, the analyses are so strikingly different that no common conclusions have emerged." *Introduction to the Old Testament as Scripture*, (Philadelphia: Fortress, 1979), 430.
4. Andersen, *Micah: A New Translation with Introduction and Commentary*, 509.

consists of a summons to judge, an accusation, a narration of the deeds by the respective parties, and a final verdict. All these elements occur in verses 1 to 8. Verses 1 to 2 state that the Lord has a legal case against his people and calls for witnesses to arise. Verses 3 to 5 recall the actions of the two parties; whereas Israel complains about being weary, the Lord has been faithful in delivering and guiding his people since the exodus from Egypt. The final verdict occurs in verses 6 to 8; the Lord's people must be reconciled to him, i.e. they need to restore the covenant relationship by righteous living.

In verses 1 and 2 the prophet, by means of personification, calls upon the mountains and hills to act as witnesses against Israel. He uses much repetition to emphasize his point. The geographical landmarks recall the historical experiences of Israel during the exodus from Egypt and entrance into Canaan as they journeyed by mountains, valleys, seas, and rivers. They experienced God's amazing acts of salvation and protection in many geographical locations outside and inside the Promised Land. In particular, the mountains of Sinai, Moab, Nebo, Ebal, Gerizim, Carmel, and Zion were locations where God spoke and acted for the sake of his covenant people. These landmarks remind Israel of God's grace and the debt they owe to their Savior and Protector. Indeed, the church father Origen correctly referred to the land of Israel as the "Fifth Gospel."

Although the literary genre of the prophetic speech is the law court scene, one should not overlook the intense emotional appeal of the language. The Lord is dismayed – even exasperated – and urges his people to contend with him. It seems that Israel simply does not care; they are neither hot nor cold. The Lord's anger over the unfaithfulness of his people demonstrates his love for them. Isn't it reasonable that a faithful and loving husband would be upset if his wife is unfaithful? Isn't it proper for loving parents to expect their children to love them in return for parental concern and toil? Loving husbands and caring parents will certainly get very upset if their loved ones behave cold-heartedly towards them. Their anger is not only justified, but also expresses deep love. In the same way, although Israel has acted as an adulterous wife and as a recalcitrant child, the Lord has not given up on his covenant people, but will continue to "contend with Israel." Israel should recognize the inappropriateness of her behavior, respond to the Lord's invitation to reason together, and be reconciled immediately. Something should be done urgently to rectify the breach in relationship. In fact, the name "Israel" means "contending" or "struggling" with God. In other words, out of love the Lord calls upon his people to live up to their name! They have to take up their complaint with

God, if they have any; and if they have reason or justice on their side, God will relent, like he relented when Jacob struggled with him until the blessing was received (Gen 32:22–32). The expression "my people," occurring twice (vv. 3 and 5), is covenantal language and shows that God has not rejected Israel. Even though the Israelites have breached the covenant, God still regards them as his people. It is also significant to note the frequent use of God's personal covenant name, "Yahweh," in this section, which again emphasizes that God has not rejected his people but wants to revive the covenant relationship he has with them. The questions highlight that God's requirements in the Mosaic covenant have not been unreasonable or excessive.

God's two questions addressed to his people invite reflection and reaction (v. 3). The first question, "What have I done to you?" implies that some were complaining that God treated them unfairly. However, further study of Israel's history reveals that there is no basis for their complaint. In fact, the verb "to do" (*'asah*) which is used here, is frequently used in Scripture to describe God's wonderful deeds of salvation and protection for his people (e.g. Exod 14:13, 31; 15:11; 19:4; Num 14:11, 22; Deut 1:30; 3:34; 4:34; Pss 18:50; 66:16; 71:19; 72:18; 77:14; 98:1; 103:6, 10). The second question, "How have I burdened you?" implies that some were complaining that God's demands were too difficult or unreasonable. In fact, according to Isaiah, God's people are wearisome to God (Isa 1:14; 7:13), and later, according to Jeremiah, they are wearing themselves out because of their sin (Jer 9:4). Rather, the following two verses point out that God has been very gracious to them and cannot be accused of being unfaithful or distant. Verse 4 shows that the prophet has the Mosaic covenant in mind. Due to his covenant faithfulness, God delivered his people from Egypt (see Exod 2:23–25). God acted for the sake of Israel on numerous occasions leading them out of Egypt, providing for them in their desert wanderings, and bringing them into the Promised Land. In addition, God raised up many prophets, men and women, to guide them along the way.[5] These leaders are an indication of God's good will towards his people. Even now too, with the prophets of the eighth century, including Micah, God is telling his people that he has not abandoned them. The presence and ministry of God's servants among Israel are in fact signs of his faithfulness.

---

5. It is interesting to note that Micah includes Miriam, a woman, among the eminent leaders God had raised up for his people in the past. We may also point to many other women in the Old Testament (like Eve, Sarah, Rebekah, Leah, Rachel, Naomi, Ruth, Hannah, Deborah, Jael, and Esther), whom God used mightily for his purposes. The role of women in the Old Testament is much more prominent than in other collections of ancient literature.

In verse 5 God calls on his people to remember their past. The command "remember" reminds the reader of Deuteronomy 8, where Moses warned the Israelites not to abandon God in prosperity, but always to remember their humble beginnings. In the Bible, remembering involves the internal mental processes of recall and meditation, as well as the outward expression of confession and proclamation. Unfortunately, Israel did not heed Moses' instructions, so when the economy prospered during the eighth century the nation forgot its history, became arrogant, and began to worship other gods. The example of Balak and Balaam recalls the story of how God works against those who oppose Israel; God frustrates plans against his people so that they come to nothing.[6] God will continue to protect the Israelites against enemies in their current context if they remember and return to him. There are many examples of how God protected his people from the evil plans of enemies in the Bible as well as in church history. In the context of Micah's time, perhaps the best biblical example is the siege of Jerusalem by Sennacherib during the time of Hezekiah in the year 701 BC. The geographical references to Shittim, the last camp before the Israelites entered Canaan (Josh 2:1; 3:1), and Gilgal, the first camp after the crossing of the Jordan (Josh 4:19–20), refer to the journey from the desert into the Promised Land.

These events happened so that God's people may "know the righteous acts of the LORD." The Hebrew wording is very significant. First of all, "knowledge" does not just mean an intellectual apprehension of something; it describes concrete experience that leads to deep understanding, passionate feeling, acknowledgment, and celebration. The expression "the righteous acts of the LORD" is a crucial theological emphasis in the Bible. "Righteousness" does not only describe an attribute of God, it also describes what God does for his people in history. In fact, the key idea behind the meaning of righteousness in the Bible is that of relationship. Because God had a covenant relationship with his people, he was faithful to them throughout history, and for their sake would often break into history to save them. Of course, it is also this understanding of righteousness that lies behind the New Testament use of the term (compare Rom 1:17). Therefore, the prophet employs Old Testament history as an educational tool to teach Israel about the nature and actions of God.

---

6. The historicity of Balaam as an ancient prophet is corroborated by the archaeological discovery of an eighth century BC inscription referring to the activities of Balaam in 1967 at Deir Alla in Jordan. See B. G. Wood, "Prophecy of Balaam found in Jordan," *Bible and Spade* 6 (1977), 121–124; M. Dijkstra, "Is Balaam also among the Prophets?" *JBL* 114 (1995), 43–64.

Micah 6–7: The Message of Reconciliation

In verses 1 to 5 the prophet established that God is above reproach, but that Israel stands condemned. The Israelites have acted in ways that have been irrational, deceitful, and disobedient. What then is to be done? After the breach of relationship (2 Kgs 18:12; Hos 8:1), what should Israel do now? The following section, verses 6 to 8, provides the verdict or the answer. With a number of rhetorical questions, the prophet establishes that ritual sacrifice is of no use. It is obvious that the answer to these rhetorical questions is a loud and resounding "no!" Several other Old Testament texts expressed the same sentiment (see for example 1 Sam 15:22; Pss 40:6–8; 51:16–17; Isa 1:11; Hos 6:6; 8:11–13; Amos 5:21–23; Mal 1:10). The early readers of the book of Micah probably would recall the thousands of animals that Hezekiah sacrificed at the cleansing of the temple (2 Chr 29:20–34; 30:19–24). But, of course, the Old Testament sacrificial practices were only an outward ritual to teach the important spiritual lesson that the human being is unholy and needs purification to approach God. Without sincerity, remorse, faith, and righteous living, the sacrifices, similar to the sacraments today, were meaningless and ineffectual. Like the author of the Letter to the Hebrews, the prophets knew that "it is impossible for the blood of bulls and goats to take away sins" (Heb 10:4). Rather, the reality of the Old Testament sacrificial system is found in Jesus' sacrifice on the cross "once and for all" (Heb 7:27; 9:11–12; 25–28; 10:10) which inaugurated the New Covenant (Luke 22:20; Heb 8:7–13; 10:16–18). It is this New Covenant that will produce changed hearts and righteous living for the coming of God's kingdom on earth. Therefore, even back in the Old Testament, the prophets already expressed a sophisticated theology of atonement (compare Ps 51:16–17; Isa 53).

In verse 8, Micah tells the reader what God demands from his people, and, according to Micah, God has already clearly told Israel what he requires. The other eighth century prophets in the Book of the Twelve also announced similar injunctions (see Hos 4:1–2; 6:6; 12:6; Amos 5:15, 24), which reflect the emphasis found in the Pentateuch (Gen 18:19; Deut 6:4–9; 10:12–21; 16:18–20; Exod 23:1–9; compare Ps 106:3; Isa 56:1; 1 Kgs 3:6; 10:9). Noticeably, the prophet is correct to point out that God's intention for his people is not new, but has been revealed to them. In addition, the language does not just lay down God's requirement for Israel, but for all people. The expression "O mortal" (literally, "O man") is generic and includes everyone. So too, according to Alfaro, "The term 'man' serves to generalize and universalize the scope of the divine directive."[7] Correspondingly, in the last requirement the general term "God" is used, rather than the more specific covenant name "Yahweh." Therefore, although the book of Micah mainly challenges the people of Israel, all people are in fact addressed (Mic 1:2), all are responsible to God (Mic 5:15), and all will experience either God's judgment or God's salvation (Mic 7:11–17).

God's demands are defined in terms of what is "good." The Hebrew term "good" (*tob*) is frequently used in the Old Testament and carries a range of meanings. According to Harris, Archer, and Waltke, it may designate (1) economic good, (2) pleasantness or beauty, (3) quality, (4) moral goodness, (5) or philosophical good.[8] The term occurs four times in Micah. In Micah 1:12 the term is used for material or physical well-being, whereas in Micah 3:2 it refers to moral goodness. In Micah 7:4 the term is used to refer to the "best" among Israel, where the idea of quality or status appears to be understood. Here in Micah 6:8, the successive statements regarding justice and mercy indicate that the term, like in Micah 3:2, is morally defined. "Goodness" consists in behavior, especially how one treats others. The verb "to require" or "to seek" (*darash*) in the next rhetorical question, "what is the LORD seeking from you?" also shows that God actually expects to find these qualities or behavioral patterns among his people. It is not just an ideal. Hebrew has two common words for "to seek," *darash* (drs) and *bikesh* (bks), which are often used synonymously. However, a word study reveals that sometimes, according to the context of Scripture, *darash* is used when the seeker finds or is expected to find the object being sought (e.g. Gen 9:5; Exod 18:15; Deut 4:29; 12:5; 19:18; Ps 34:5, 10; Isa 1:17; 55:6; Amos 5:4, 6), whereas *bikesh* is frequently used in contexts where the seeker does not find or is not able to reach the intended goal (e.g. Gen 39:15–16; Exod 2:15; 4:19, 24; Deut 4:29; 13:11; Josh 2:22; 1 Sam 23:14; Pss 35:4; 37:32, 36; Isa 41:12–13; 45:19; Jer 5:1; Hos 2:9; 5:6; Amos 8:12). Therefore, the use of the word *darash* here further indicates that justice, mercy, and humility are not just sentiments for intellectual consent, but are meant to be expressed in practical living. The emphasis is clearly on behavior, and not on a set of beliefs. This is a good reminder for us today that God is more concerned about how we live as Christians – how we treat others – than on the finer points of our theology.

---

7. Alfaro, *Justice and Loyalty: A Commentary on the Book of Micah*, 69.
8. Laird R. Harris, L. Gleason Archer, and Bruce K. Waltke, *Theological Wordbook of the Old Testament*. 2 volumes (Chicago: Moody Press, 1980), 345–346.

Micah 6–7: The Message of Reconciliation

God's requirement is expressed in terms of a question, which invites a response from the listener. Every listener is forced to answer the interrogation, to agree or disagree, to accept or to reject. And it is hardly possible for anyone to answer "no;" it is then only a matter of practice. Those who live according to the requirements will be exonerated and blessed; those who do not, have condemned themselves through their own answer and conscience. God is indeed above reproach and every sinner stands self-condemned (see Rom 2:1–11). People need to do three things, "to act justly and to love mercy and to walk humbly with your God." The three elements highlight separate requirements, but are also closely related. One element leads to, or depends on, the succeeding one; they form a coherent picture of the godly life. If one element is missing, the others become meaningless.[9]

Thus, the last requirement "godliness," even though perhaps the most important, is hollow without the first two, "justice" and "kindness." Love for God, the first table of the law, is conditioned by love for one's fellow human being, the second table of the law. As the apostle John taught his disciples, "Whoever claims to love God yet hates a brother or sister is a liar. For whoever does not love their brother and sister, whom they have seen, cannot love God, whom they have not seen" (1 John 4:20). Again, we should note that the text does not merely list some legal requirements, but rather demands intimate relationship, deep emotional feeling, and sincere action; it is more like a marriage relationship than a business association.

The first aspect of a good life is "to act justly" or "to do justice," which describes one's duty with respect to others. The word "justice" (*mispat*) is a very important term in the Old Testament. It occurs 424 times and covers all aspects of human conduct, whether in business, courts, family, friendship, strangers, or society. From its root meaning of "decision" or "judgment" a number of nuances is conveyed by the term including, legal decision, sentence (the decision of a judge), the execution of judgment, proper measure, right, and justice. According to the *International Standard Bible Encyclopedia*, "In a larger sense justice is not only giving to others their rights, but involves the active duty of establishing their rights."[10] It is one of the frequently mentioned attributes of God; God loves justice (Pss 33:5; 37:38; 99:4) and he acts justly (Ps 111:7). Thus, a major concern expressed in the Mosaic covenant was that

---

9. For Limburg, there is a "step-by-step escalation" (*Hosea-Micah. Interpretation: A Bible Commentary for Teaching and Preaching*, 191).
10. Harris Franklin Rall, "Justice," in *International Standard Bible Encyclopaedia. Vol. 3*. James Orr, ed.(Chicago: The Howard Severance Company, 1915), 1781.

Israel's judges should act justly (Exod 23:1–9; Deut 16:18–20). It was of such a great concern that the High Priest had to carry a breastplate on his chest with the words, "breastplate of justice" (Exod 28:15, 29–30). In the prophets, the term gains special prominence against the background of the exploitation of the poor and not giving them their legal rights (see Isa 1:17). One big complaint of Micah's was that Israel's leaders did not afford justice to the poor (Mic 3:1).

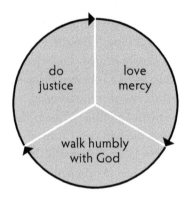

The second aspect of a good life is "to love mercy," which describes one's inner demeanor towards compassion as well as outward acts of kindness. The word translated "kindness" (*hesed*) occurs 255 times and is one of the most significant theological words in the Old Testament. It is perhaps the attribute of God that is most emphasized in the Bible and is closely related to God's covenant faithfulness (see Exod 15:13; 20:6; 34:6–7; Num 14:18–19; Deut 7:9; Neh 9:17, 32; Ezra 3:11; Pss 5:7; 69:13; 86:15; 103:8; 136; 145:8; Isa 54:8–10; 63:7; Jer 9:23–24; Joel 2:13; Mic 7:18). As with justice, the Israelites must reflect God's kindness in their relationship with others. However, in the eighth century Israel lacked kindness; society became callous and mean (Hos 4:1; 6:4; see also Jonah 2:8). The stress in Micah is that people should "love" kindness. Whereas justice must be done, kindness must be cherished. With justice the emphasis is on the outer expression of non-discriminatory action; with kindness the emphasis is on an inner attitude of compassion towards those who need help.

The third aspect of a good life is "to walk humbly with your God," which describes one's attitude with respect to God. The command "to walk" (*halach*) according to the Lord's commandments occurs frequently in the Mosaic covenant (see Deut 5:33; 10:12; 13:4; 26:17), but it was already used to describe Enoch, Noah, and the patriarchs' relationship with God before the giving of the Mosaic Law (Gen 5:22, 24; 6:9; 17:1; 24:40; 48:15). Therefore, the expression implies more than walking according to the detailed stipulations of God's laws; more importantly, it denotes a life of trusting relationship with the Lord. It means a spiritual orientation or a heart commitment of love and trust towards God. This spiritual orientation is frequently expressed in the desire of the psalmist for an intimate relationship with God (Pss 86:11; 119:1–3). In the eighth century we read that the kings of Israel and Judah did not walk in God's ways, but followed the customs of the surrounding nations (2 Kgs 16:3; 17:8, 19, 22). When God is no longer the central orientation of one's life, other things quickly fill the void. In Micah, the command is further illuminated with the adverb "humbly," which contrasts with the rich and powerful who "walk haughtily" (Mic 2:3). Those who walk humbly with the Lord put aside their own agendas and make the Lord's concerns the center of their lives (see 2 Sam 22:28; 2 Chr 7:14; Pss 18:27; 25:9; 149:4; Prov 16:19; Isa 57:15; 66:2; Zeph 2:3). We also noted that in the great vision of future restoration, the motivation of the Gentiles for coming to Jerusalem would be to walk in the "ways of the LORD" (Mic 4:2, 5). It is indeed this final aspect of God's requirements that supplies the motivation and power to do justice and to love mercy. Alfaro commented, "In Mic 6:8 the prophet has presented a perfect summary of the biblical religion found frequently in the Prophets. True religion must be a means for an encounter with God and with others, and must not become an end in itself and for itself."[11] The New Testament definition or understanding of godliness in James 1:26–27 comes very close to this text in Micah.

---

11. Alfaro, *Justice and Loyalty: A Commentary on the Book of Micah*, 69.

GENUINE REPENTANCE IS REQUIRED

The prophetic message of Micah is a serious invitation to Christians today to consider whether God may have a grievance against them. So too, Paul in the New Testament calls upon Christians to examine themselves to see whether they are real Christians (Gal 6:4; 1 Cor 11:28; 2 Cor 13:5). It is very easy to be self-deceived and to assume that everything is well (Jer 17:9). The state of the church, the decadence of society, and the degradation of the environment shout loudly to us that everything is not well. These are signs, according to the book of Revelation, for the world and especially for Christians to wake up, to repent, and to return to God. In the *Analects*, "Master Zeng said: Each day I examine myself upon three points. In planning for others, have I been loyal? In company with friends, have I been trustworthy? And have I practiced what has been passed on to me?" (1.4).[1] How much more, should the Christian, having received the revelation of God, be anxious to live a righteous and honest life?

Micah 6:6–8 is a good yardstick for self-examination. Where have our attitudes and actions been selfish, biased, and unjust? James, the brother of the Lord, noted, "Religion that God our Father accepts as pure and faultless is this: to look after orphans and widows in their distress and to keep oneself from being polluted by the world" (Jas 1:27). Do we love to be kind and are we eager to help the poor? How much money do we spend on ourselves and our church buildings in comparison with helping those in desperate need? Do we walk before God in reverence? Of course, we cannot abide perfectly by these requirements and that is why we need the mercy and forgiveness of Jesus. Nevertheless, the Christian must reflect these qualities in some measure. If they are altogether missing, then we may well conclude that we are still far away from God's kingdom (Matt 7:21–23).

Evangelical Christians usually emphasize holy living which we equate with not getting drunk, not taking drugs, not robbing banks, not visiting prostitutes, and not engaging in homosexual practices. Of course, we should abstain from these vices, but we often turn a blind eye to injustice, unkindness, and prejudice. Micah never castigates the Israelites for drunkenness or prostitution; rather he exposes the greater sins of injustice and exploitation. In fact, sometimes injustice and meanness may do much more harm to others and the reputation of the church than the lusts of the flesh. The word of God must correct our assumptions and values. It appears that God is not very interested in the "theology" of the Israelites (e.g. Calvinism or Arminianism) or how much they have offered to God (e.g. size of their donations), rather God is more concerned about how they treat others, whether they help the poor, and what attitudes they have in their hearts before God. Likewise, in the New Testament, Jesus similarly reprimanded the Pharisees for being hypocrites; preferring human honors and wealth over justice, mercy, and sincere faith (see Matt 23). God does not want us just to be Christians in name, but Christians in behavior.

The prophet Jonah is a good illustration of the kind of behavior that Micah wants to expose. Jonah is a typical representative of Israel; there is no problem with his confession of faith and his understanding of God, he declared, "I am a Hebrew and I worship the Lord, the God of heaven, who made the sea and the dry land" (Jonah 1:9), and "you are a gracious and compassionate God, slow to anger and abounding in love, a God who relents from sending calamity" (Jonah 4:2). Yet, Jonah's behavior with respect to God's heart and the plight of the Gentiles is entirely incompatible with his theological knowledge. He did not care for the lives of the sailors in the storm or for the well-being of the Ninevites in the face of impending judgment. He was more concerned about his own theological agenda and physical comfort than the plight of the lost or the depths of God's tender mercies. Sadly, God's people often behave like the prophet Jonah. We may recall the life of Ivan the Terrible (1530–1584), the Russian Tsar, who regularly prayed for three hours every morning in his chapel, but then tortured his critics to death in the afternoon. Unfortunately, such inconsistent behavior also occurs in the Asian church. A rural pastor in Asia after learning about the five points of Calvinism returned to his church and introduced his new knowledge as the five golden lights to illuminate the whole Bible. Every biblical passage was interpreted through this grid and when some members expressed some reservations they were immediately excommunicated. The church split in two, families became enemies, and the church lost any credible witness and became notorious for disunity in the village. One of the worst things a pastor can do is to split a church and pull congregational members along with him when he leaves to serve in another location. Jesus used the analogy of ravenous wolves to describe those who tear God's flock apart. Sadly, we often see such behavior by pastors and leaders in Asian churches today.

---

1. R. Eno, *The Analects of Confucius*, 2015, 1.

6:9–16 God's Verdict on the City

The second half of the chapter announces God's verdict and judgment upon his people. More particularly, whereas the first half of the chapter addresses the people of Judah in general, the second half addresses the city of Jerusalem. Since, the "city" in verse 9 is compared with the wicked counsels of Omri and Ahab, the kings of Samaria, there is not much doubt that Jerusalem is in view here. Judgment has already fallen on the northern kingdom; the last warnings are now given to the capital city of Judah. In the Hebrew text, the clause translated as "the LORD is calling" is literally "the voice of the LORD," which is a standard expression found in the Old Testament occurring frequently in Deuteronomy (5:25; 8:20; 13:18; 15:5; 18:16; 26:14; 27:10; 28:1, 2, 15, 45, 62; 30:8, 10). It was the first sound that Adam and Eve heard after they ate the forbidden fruit (Gen 3:8). The use of the expression emphasizes that God's requirements have been made clear to his people. They are no longer in the dark about them and cannot plead ignorance. In the context here, the voice of the Lord refers to the message of Micah about impending judgment and the need to repent. Those who consider the message carefully, take it to heart, and fear the Lord will indeed be wise. "The rod" is an instrument of discipline and refers to the calamities that Israel has already begun to experience as the result of disobedience.[12] Just as a father does not overlook bad behavior in his children, but disciplines them so that they may amend their ways and be upright and blessed (Prov 13:24; 22:15; 23:13; 29:17), so too God is disciplining his people (Lev 26:18–28; 2 Sam 7:14; Ps 94:10; Prov 3:11; Hos 5:2; 7:12; 10:10). The calamities that have fallen upon them did not happen by chance, but came from the loving hand of God to correct his covenant people.

According to the words of the denunciation, injustice and deceit are everywhere and God cannot put up with it any longer. The rhetorical questions in verses 11 and 12 draw the listener into the conservation; he or she cannot remain aloof or be a neutral bystander. Scales and weights are supposed to measure quantities accurately, however here they are intentionally designed to do just the opposite. In the Bible, inaccurate weights are regarded as morally "wicked" and "deceitful" (see Prov 11:1; 20:23). Whereas these commercial operators may look at it as shrewd business practice, God regards it as a grave sin. Archaeological discoveries of ancient stone weights with wide differences of mass illustrate the point that Micah is making (see Figure 18). Waltke also noted that, "Ancient balances had a margin of error of up to six percent, and archaeologists have found few weights inscribed with the same denomination to be of exactly identical weight, so only approximate modern equivalents can be given."[13] The symbolism does not just refer to the commercial world, but to all areas of social activity.

---

12. Micah's use of the Hebrew word *mateh* for "rod" instead of the more usual word *shebet* (Prov 10:13; 13:24; 22:15; 23:13–14; 29:15) may be due to his agricultural context. A *mateh* was used as a farming implement to herd sheep or to thresh the grain (Lev 27:32; Isa 28:27).
13. Waltke, *Micah: An Introduction and Commentary*, 197.

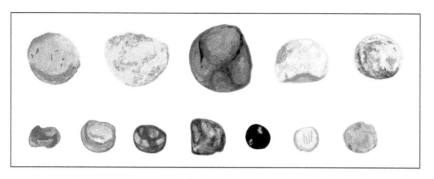

Figure 18. Stone Weights from the First Temple period
(The Temple Mount Sifting Project)

The same Hebrew term "deceitful" (*mirma*) is also used in the Psalms to describe words that are not honest but harbor evil intent (Pss 50:19; 52:6; 109:2). The psalmist prays that God may protect him from speaking deceitful words (Pss 17:1; 34:14). The Chinese proverb, "Hang out a goat's head, while selling dog's meat" (挂羊头，卖狗肉), articulates the same deceitful behavior in the commercial world. But, it is again important to note that Micah is not describing the pagan world of Israel's surroundings, but is painting a picture of the covenant community. Judah had become a "dog eats dog" society. God's children have forgotten who they are and are ignoring God's purpose for saving them and bringing them into the Promised Land. Therefore, according to verse 13, God has already brought misadventure upon them. The Hebrew verb literally means "to make weak" or "to make sick," and is expressed in the perfect tense which is roughly equivalent to the English past tense. Thus, the text is not describing the future, but what has already fallen upon the people.[14] They have to interpret these calamities correctly and recognize that their difficulties have not come upon them due to chance, the Assyrians, or some foul water; rather, they are due to their deceitful behavior.

Verses 14 to 15 describe the emptiness of life in an unjust and corrupt society, despite much activity and superficial prosperity. Outwardly things seem to be going well, but inwardly there is a spike in hopelessness and depressive illnesses. People's busyness for worldly things do not bring lasting joy, it is like "chasing wind and catching shadows" (捕风捉影) or like "grasping for the moon in water" (水中捞月). All these idolatrous pursuits will be

---

14. Many versions translate the perfect as a prophetic perfect indicating the future. However, according to the context, it seems that the past perfect is more appropriate.

fruitless. Perhaps the most terrifying judgment is to permit the wicked to get what they seek (see Rom 1:24–25). The glutton will eventually be destroyed by consumption, the drunkard by intoxication, the promiscuous by venereal disease, and the greedy by avarice. People whose only aim is to build bigger barns and acquire larger estates will be disappointed. Their life's work will pass on to others or disappear into smoke. There are frequent warnings in the wisdom traditions of Israel concerning the dangers of greed (Pss 39:6; 62:10; Prov 11:4, 7, 16, 28; 13:11; 22:16; 23:3–5; 27:24; Eccl 5:10; 9:11–12). Instead, the biblical ideal is to live a quiet and wholesome life, being content with modest means, and to share with those in need (Prov 30:8; Eccl 5:18–20; 8:15; 9:7–10; Luke 12:15; 1 Tim 6:6–10).

Our current situation appears to be very similar to Judean society in Micah's time. Although Asia is currently not experiencing war, people are awfully empty within because they worship money and materialism. The religions around them cannot not bring peace and joy. Since there is an absence of absolute standards, moral decay has become rampant. Unscrupulous businessmen are even prepared to adulterate food for the sake of making a quick profit. In some parts of Asia, milk has been mixed with melamine, unhygienic oil from gutters is used for cooking, and diseased meat and vegetables laced with pesticides are sold to innocent consumers. People can only sigh in exasperation, not knowing what is safe to eat. Greed is destroying the well-being of ordinary people, causing much cynicism and hopelessness.

Figure 19. The Mesha Stelea, also known as the Moabite Stone, dates from the 8th century BC and refers to King Omri (Louvre Museum)

Micah 6–7: The Message of Reconciliation

Figure 20. The seal of King Ahab (Hecht Museum)

The last verse of the oracle gives the final reason for failure and widespread discontent in Judean society; the people of the southern kingdom have become like their northern brothers and sisters. Omri, and especially his son, Ahab, were notorious for being the worst kings of Israel (1 Kgs 16:25, 30–33; 21:15; 2 Kgs 8:18; 2 Chr 22:3). Ahab married the notorious idolater Jezebel (1 Kgs 16:31), increased pagan worship in Israel (1 Kgs 21), and persecuted the Lord's prophets (1 Kgs 18:1–18). Yet, here Micah is saying that the people of Jerusalem are no better than Omri and Ahab, but are the same as these most wicked kings in Israel's history. If the leaders of Judah do not immediately repent and amend their wicked practices the same judgment is going to fall upon them. This verse also reveals that the last section of the book of Micah is addressed to Judah, since the northern kingdom no longer exists.

Figure 21. The view towards Moresheth from Gath

The church may provide a beacon of hope in Asia. If Christian workers, businessmen, and church leaders embrace God's concern for righteousness and integrity, there will be a powerful resurgence of hope. Instead of engaging in political activities to undermine existing regimes or follow the *status quo* to enrich themselves, Christians should take practical action to live lives and run businesses that demonstrate the values of God's kingdom: honesty, righteousness, justice, and mercy.

MICAH AND PREACHING

In what way is Micah's message different from that of the false prophets? What did he preach and how did he convey his message? What can we learn from Micah about preaching? The answers to these questions are very relevant for preachers and teachers today.

First of all, we may examine the content of Micah's message. According to our analysis of the book, Micah made three main points or had three emphases in his preaching. In general, one-third of his prophecy or sermon was on Israel's past sin and on judgment (section one: chapters 1-3); one-third was on future restoration and hope (section two: chapters 4-5); and one-third was on the need for reconciliation with God in the present time (section three: chapters 6-7). Micah did not shy away from exposing the sins of God's people, and especially emphasized injustices, greed, and corruption within the covenant community. Consequently, he announced severe judgment upon Israel. In fact, God's judgment has already begun through the Assyrian threat and plundering of Israelite towns. It is likely that most of Micah's ministry took place after the fall of Samaria and the northern exile. According to Micah, these events were not random political developments, but God's judgment upon Israel's sin. But while Micah exposed Israel's sin, he also painted a bright picture of future restoration, providing much hope for God's beleaguered people. This restoration would take place through God's coming reign in the person of the ruler from Bethlehem. God's people were going to be refined, gathered and restored, and would become a blessing to the world. However, Micah's last point, the restoration must be preceded by repentance and trust in the Lord. Therefore, Micah urged his hearers to return to the Lord, to amend their lives, and to live in the reality of the future. God would forgive their sins and fulfill the promises of the Abrahamic covenant. In short, Micah's sermon follows the general framework of salvation history as presented in the overall narrative of the canon.

In addition, observing some further details in his sermon, Micah often recalled events from Israel's history and reminded his readers of the Lord's covenant faithfulness. Many themes stem from elements in the Abrahamic, Mosaic, and Davidic covenants. Micah was a keen student of Israel's history. But also, and perhaps more importantly, Micah had a forward orientation; greater things were going to happen in the future. In a way, one may say that there is more emphasis on the future of salvation history than on the past. Micah was not just calling people to remember the past and to return to the stipulations of the covenant, he encouraged his hearers to wait expectantly for a glorious restoration that would be even more significant than the great events of the past. God was going to do greater things in the future: the restoration of Zion, the gathering of the remnant, and the establishment of global peace.

In this message of future restoration, most weight is placed on the coming ruler from Bethlehem, or we may say, on the person and work of the Messiah.[1] Indeed, the whole book of Micah, according to its canonical context, is saturated with allusions, references, and prophecies about Jesus. For example, in chapter 1, the first words of the prophecy "The Word of the Lord" (1:1) points to the clearest revelation of God in Jesus (John 1:1–18; 2 Tim 4:8), the expression "the Lord is coming" (Mic 1:3) is fulfilled in the ministry of Jesus (Mark 1:2–3), and the message of coming judgment reminds us that Jesus is the judge of the world (Acts 17:31). In Micah 2:12–13, the prophecy about the Lord being Israel's deliverer, shepherd, and king is fulfilled in the work of Jesus (e.g. John 10:1–16). Micah 4:1–4 looks to the messianic age which was inaugurated with the coming of Jesus into the world (Mark 1:14–15), and the statement in Micah 4:7 that the "Lord will reign" is also a reference to the messianic kingdom (Luke 1:33; Rev 11:15). In Micah 4:8 the Messiah is directly addressed in the imagery about the pains and joys of child birth. Micah 4:9–10 is applied in the New Testament to the cross and resurrection of Jesus (John 16:20–24), and the victory portrayed in Micah 4:13 is achieved through the Messiah (compare Pss 2, 110). In chapter 5 the prophecy about the coming ruler is of course fulfilled in Jesus being born in Bethlehem, and the portrayal of God's people being a blessing throughout the world in Micah 5:7–15 is a description of the church age (Matt 13:14-35; Rev 5:10; 20:6). In Micah 6:5, "the righteous acts of the Lord" (Mic 6:5) refers especially to Jesus' redemptive activity (Matt 3:15; Acts 3:14; 7:52; Rom 1:17), whereas the requirements of Micah 6:8 are perfectly demonstrated in Jesus' life (Matt 9:35-36; 11:2–6). In Micah 7:8 the expression "the Lord will be my light" reminds us that Jesus is the light of the world (John 1:4–5; 8:12), and in Micah 7:8, 11–12 we have another depiction of the future messianic or church age. Micah 7:14 is fulfilled in Jesus as the good shepherd (Heb 13:20; 1 Pet 2:25) and, of course, the marvelous doxology in Micah 7:18–20 is perfectly illustrated in the person and work of Christ in the gospel. Using the terminology of New Testament theology, we may say that Micah's preaching was Christocentric.

Therefore, the content of Micah's preaching provides much instruction for preachers today. Preachers and teachers may examine their own teaching and ascertain how it corresponds to the content of Micah's message and emphases. For Christians, the Scriptures are the highest authority and are normative in every area relating to doctrine and life; so certainly, the Scriptures should also govern what we preach and teach today. One of the main differences between false prophets and true prophets is that the former teach their own ideas whereas the latter teach God's truth. If Micah is our model, then preachers need to be more courageous and forthright to expose the church's sin. They may also carefully and sensitively consider whether political upheaval, economic crises, and natural disasters – which occur regularly throughout Asia – are the judgments of God upon wickedness and injustice.

The book of Micah also encourages preachers today to examine their messages in terms of salvation history and Christ-centeredness. The main narrative of Micah's sermon is salvation history – what God is doing in history for the salvation of his people – which culminates in the person and work of Jesus. It is a sad fact that there is not much understanding of salvation history and the centrality of the gospel in Asian churches today. Most preaching and teaching are about ideas for better living or ways to achieve healing, success, and happiness. While there is a place for such themes to be explored from the pulpit and in Bible studies, they are not the central concerns of the biblical message. According to Martin Luther, every generation needs to have a new and fresh discovery of the gospel. Jesus is the "Alpha and the Omega," he is the center of salvation history, the center of all biblical revelation and teaching, and in him all the fullness of God resides. These are radical views in today's world and are often not warmly received – even in some Christian circles – yet, these convictions are the emphases of biblical truth and the basis of discipleship. Micah may assist Asian preachers and teachers to rediscover the gospel and center their messages on the cross and resurrection of Jesus. Finally, preachers may also learn from Micah's urgent call to be reconciled to God, to amend their lives, and to embrace both suffering and hope. Indeed, with such repentance, Christians may be confident that God will bring about the beautiful reign of peace in their own lives, churches, and societies.[2]

Another question that concerns preachers and teachers is how to present God's word to people? Again, Micah's example is instructive and may provide a model for the way we preach and teach today. Firstly, we observe that roughly a third of Micah's sermon may be classified as teaching, a third consists of illustration, and another third may be placed under the category of application.[3] Micah moves to-and-fro from one category to another, keeping the hearers alert and engaged. His teaching or theological statements are amply illustrated with a rich variety of stories from Israel's history and many nature metaphors. Micah often refers to events, places, and people known from the Scriptures

Micah 6–7: The Message of Reconciliation

to augment his points. It also appears that the prophet employed examples from current political events and issues in society to illustrate his teaching; he was well-informed about contemporary affairs and addressed them. He used a lot of imagery from elements in agriculture and nature, things which would have been familiar to Micah's rural audience. Micah's application is interspersed throughout his discourse and is filled with passionate persuasion. The sermon expresses rapid and contrasting shifts in emotion; there are fear, anxiety, and despair, but also excitement, confidence, and joy. Finally, in line with its poetic style, the prophecy is filled with literary devices such as parallelism, repetition, hyperbole, alliteration, and play on words. Obviously, Micah, and subsequently the book's editors, spent much time in crafting the message for optimum clarity and effect.

Preachers today may learn from the techniques Micah used in his prophecy. Firstly, preachers and teachers should vary their content in terms of teaching, illustration, and application. We often spend too much time on articulating theology without enough illustrations and application, which make sermons boring and irrelevant. According to the example of Micah, the stories of the Bible and nature provide a rich treasure trove of illustrations. Preachers and teachers also need to be in touch with the local news and world events in order to address current issues. Since God always has a word for his people in their specific contexts, every area, every city, and every church needs to have its own "prophet" to guide God's people in their distinctive setting. And, finally, preachers must spend much time in studying, in interpreting, in prayer, and in preparation to communicate God's word to their constituencies. In fact, the main task of preachers is to teach God's word. Therefore, most of their time and effort should be focused on studying and proclaiming God's word to the church and to the world, rather than on meetings and administration.

---

1. Although Micah does not use the term "Messiah," his prophecies about the coming deliverer are messianic since there is an exact correspondence between the person and work of the future deliverer in Micah and in other canonical texts that describe the Messiah and his kingdom (see Pss 2; 18; 45; 132; Isa 61; Dan 9:24–27).
2. In terms of preaching, readers may again find it helpful to note the suggested principles for preaching on prophecy in the Introduction.
3. Of course, this categorization depends on the criteria we use and how we apply them to the interpretation of the message of the prophet.

MICAH 7

Although it is difficult to come up with a clear outline of the subsections in chapter 7, its main theme is clear. Despite challenging personal and national circumstances, Micah expresses exuberant confidence that the Lord will deliver him and fulfill his purposes for the world. When humans find themselves in the gloomiest predicaments, God's kingdom triumphs. Therefore, those who trust in the Lord will never be disappointed.

We have divided the chapter into three parts. In the first part, the prophet Micah responds to God's verdict and judgment (vv. 1–10). The second part calls God's people to action in view of future restoration (vv. 11–17). And the final verses of the chapter act as a conclusion or doxology, not just to the chapter, but to the whole prophecy (vv. 18–20). Perhaps, the disorderly thematic structure may be a literary device the author or editor employed to reflect a chaotic society.

7:1–10 The Prophet's Second Response

In verses 1 to 10 we have the prophet Micah's response to the state of God's people as described in chapter 6. This is now the second response of the prophet in the book of Micah. Whereas the first response was at the beginning of the book of Micah (Mic 1:8–16), the second response occurs at the end of the book. The two responses of the prophet serve as two book ends and demonstrate the reaction that the prophecy wishes to evoke in the listeners. The prophet Micah serves as the model, perhaps even as a representative of the ideal Israel as Jonah served as the representative of the actual Israel, in response to God's word. In both passages there are anguish, lament, and remorse. However, in the second response there is a dramatic shift in mood from despair to hope, from sadness to jubilation, and from defeat to victory. In this way, Micah also features as a type of Christ, who although apparently defeated triumphed over all. The Hebrew expression, "Alas for me" ("What misery is mine!" NIV) occurs only once elsewhere in the Old Testament (Job 10:15) and is an instance of onomatopia (a literary device where a word mimics the sound it describes), which intensifies the emotional mood of the passage. Remarkably, the prophet considers that he himself is included among those who are sinful in chapter 6 and stands under God's judgment. There is even nothing in his own actions, he says, that he desires. The implication for the listeners is clear: if God's prophet has failed to live according to covenant expectations, how much worse would the rest of us be! Micah uses the image of a fruitless tree, something that would have been familiar from his rural surroundings, to illustrate the barrenness of his life (compare Ps 1:3). God is looking for fruit, but there is none. Upon closer examination of his life, there is no ground for satisfaction or boasting. In fact, the judgment of barrenness described in Micah 6:14–15 is already being experienced by the prophet himself. In the Old Testament, a vine or vineyard is sometimes used as a symbol for Israel (e.g. Song 2:13, 15; 7:12; Isa 5:1–4; Jer 2:21; Ezek 15:2; Hos 10:1; see also Matt 20:1–16; 21:33–46; John 15:1–8). It is also instructive to consider that the only value of the vine lies in producing grapes; it is useless for shade or timber. In other words, a fruitless vine does not fulfill any useful purpose and will be uprooted by the farmer (see Luke 13:6–9). So too, without the fruits of justice, mercy, and humility, God's people do not perform any useful function and will also be uprooted. The sentence "as the gleaning of the grapes; there is no cluster to eat" refers to the covenantal injunction not to strip the vines bare of all fruit, but to leave some behind for the poor (see Lev 19:9; 23:22; Deut 24:19–21; Ruth 2). Micah is saying that the poor are being neglected, possibly even including himself.

According to verse 2, the "faithful" or "godly" (*hasid*) (i.e. the gracious and merciful ones), are no more. Being "faithful" or "godly" is defined as being merciful, as in Micah 6:8, it is one of the central qualities that God looks for in his people (see Hos 4:1; Jonah 2:8). The term is also used elsewhere to describe the godly (2 Sam 22:26; Pss 4:4; 12:12; 18:26; 32:6; 43:1; 86:2). Whereas the first line of the verse refers to God's people, the latter line, "not one upright person remains" (literally, "and there is no upright one among humanity"), seems to describe the world. Although the book of Micah focuses on Israel, it expresses God's concern for the world. Micah's feeling is even more despairing than Elijah's, who considered that Israel had forsaken the covenant and that he alone was left (1 Kgs 19:14). For Micah, all God's people, including himself, and the whole world have fallen short of God's intention for humanity. Society has become violent, selfish, and deceitful. People excel only in evil. The leaders of society are totally corrupt and fill their own pockets at the expense of the poor. Bribes and impudence have become common place. The rich and powerful have established networks to exploit the poor and protect themselves. The best people are like a thorn bush (v. 4), they may not pursue or attack you, but they have no practical benefit and if you get close to them for help you are pricked and injured. "The day of your watchmen" refers to the day when the watchman spots the arrival of the enemy (i.e. the day of disaster or punishment has arrived). The result of this punishment is confusion. The social and business networks which people have built up for themselves are starting to collapse. The world around them no longer makes sense and has ceased to support their structures for self-enrichment and power (see Isa 22:5). It appears that the social situation Micah is describing here is worse than that in chapters 2 and 3.

In verses 5 to 6 we note that even the closest family relationships are now starting to break down. Three warnings are given not to trust even one's closest kin. There is an escalation in the degree of disloyalty from neighbors, close friends, and finally even from one's spouse. No one can be trusted. There is no loyalty in relationships; righteousness has disappeared. The foundation of every society lies in stable family structures of loyalty and support. However, this glue that holds society together is now disintegrating. A graphic example of this breakdown in family relationships is seen in the behavior of Manasseh, Hezekiah's successor, who sacrificed his own son to pagan gods (2 Kgs 21:6).[15] Families are the bedrock of society, with the break down in family relationships, orderly and functional society disintegrates. In Matthew 10:34–36, Jesus envisaged the same breakdown in family relationships due to his coming into the world.

In verses 7 to 10 the prophet returns to relate his own experience and conviction. But now, surprisingly, there is a drastic change in mood. Micah's despair turns into hope. Despite the turmoil in society, the prophet has not lost confidence, but instead rises up with assured faith in the Lord. Whereas people only see enemies and calamity, Micah sees the coming and action of God himself. In the Hebrew text the word for "watchman" in verse 4 and the verb "I watch" in verse 7 stem from the same root (*tsapha*). There is a contrast with what people see and what Micah sees. People see disaster and confusion, but Micah sees the arrival of God's salvation! In the Hebrew text, God's name, "Yahweh," stands before the verb in an emphatic position. This vision focusing on the Lord himself inspires Micah with assurance and trust. The prophet's hope resides totally in God, not in a coming king, prophet, or reformer. The sentiment expressed here, that ultimately only God can bring salvation, is the central conviction of apocalyptic thought and lies at the heart of biblical theology. God is the hope of the world.[16] The contrast with verses 5 and 6 is very pronounced; instead of trusting in people, we must trust in God (see Ps 118:7–9). The final clause "my God will hear me," which can also

---

15. The book of Micah was probably edited into its final form during the time of Manasseh (2 Kgs 21:1–18).
16. See Ted Peters, "Idolatry is not the absence of faith. It is faith in the wrong thing." *God – The World's Future: Systematic Theology for a New Era* (Minneapolis: Fortress, 2000), 27.

be translated with the present tense as "my God is hearing me," shows that Micah is sustaining his faith through the exercise of prayer.

In verse 8, Micah addresses his enemy, probably both rhetorically and in an actual historical context. He aims to encourage himself and to inspire confidence in others. We have already seen in Micah 2:6 that some people were opposing Micah, accusing him of not being a true prophet. The same people would readily interpret any misfortune in the life of the prophet as a sign of God's rejection. We may recall how Jesus' enemies mocked him on the cross. However, Micah is confident that his enemies will not have the last laugh. He may experience setbacks and fall down, but will certainly experience God's vindication and marvelous deliverance. It may also be significant to point out that the verbs in verse 8 may be translated into English as, "When I fell, I got up; when I sit in darkness, the LORD is my light." The prophet is not just articulating his future hope, but is really sharing his past and present experiences. The word "enemy" may also refer at a deeper level to the powers of evil at work in the world, opposing God's plan of salvation. It literally means "enmity" and is the same word used in Genesis 3:15, where God says that he will put "enmity" between the serpent and the woman's seed. According to the New Testament writers, God ultimately defeated the enemy of his people on the cross of Jesus (John 12:31; Rom 8:31–35; Col 2:14–15; Rev 12:7–9). The great transformation or reversal from defeat to victory, or darkness to light, is defined by the verb "to rise," which subtly recalls the summons at the beginning of the section to arise for judgment (Mic 6:1). It is a keyword in both the Old Testament and the New Testament. In the Old Testament the verb is used to describe the restoration of Israel (e.g. Isa 44:26; 49:6; 52:2; 58:12; 61:1–4; Hos 6:2), is employed in the divine call of prophets (e.g. Josh 1:2; Jer 1:17; Amos 2:11; Jonah 1:2; 3:2), and is also used in connection with the future deliverer of Israel (e.g. Deut 18:15, 18; Ezek 34:23; Amos 9:11; Zech 11:16). In the New Testament, of course, the corresponding Greek verbs are used to describe Jesus' resurrection from the dead (John 21:14; Rom 10:9; 1 Cor 6:14). Indeed, Micah's experience and hope of "resurrection" is spectacularly fulfilled in the resurrection of Jesus, which was the "first fruits" of the resurrection of all God's people scheduled for the end of the age (1 Cor 15:20). The symbolic change from darkness to light also describes the experience of death and resurrection (see also Isa 9:2; 49:9; 58:10; 60:2–3; Pss 18:28; 112:4).

In verse 9 Micah continues to reflect on his own experience, and the keywords "he pleads my case" (*rib*) link the passage with the opening summons of the section (Mic 6:1). Micah's vivid rhetoric demonstrates that God's people have breached the stipulations of covenant faithfulness and have become a wicked nation. What is to be done? Is there still any hope? Here in verse 9 the tension comes to a resolution. Sin will be punished, but more significantly, the Lord himself will come to the aid of his people and resolve the breach in covenant relationship. Whereas before God is pictured as the plaintiff and judge of his people, now amazingly he also becomes their advocate. Even though Micah sinned against the Lord, the Lord will still pick up his case and plead for him. The Lord himself will be the one doing the reconciling. Mere repentance is not enough, there also needs to be the removal of guilt. Although the prophet's wording points to the idea of vicarious atonement, the full meaning of Micah's sentiment can only be understood when the rest of biblical revelation is taken into account. Firstly, there are many verbal links to the description of the exodus from Egypt. The verbs "to establish" (*'asah*), "to bring out" (*yatsa*), and "to see" (*ra'ah*) are all key terms frequently used in the Exodus narrative (e.g. Exod 12:40–41; 14:13, 30; 15:17; Deut 4:34–38). So too, the nouns "light" and "righteousness" are also associated with Israel's exodus experience (Exod 10:23; 13:21; 14:20; Deut 6:20–25; 9:4–6). Of course, on the basis of the Passover sacrifice, God brought about for Israel the great deliverance from slavery. Secondly, the whole process of Micah's justification is summarized as "his righteousness," the possessive pronoun referring to God. In a way, Micah is a passive bystander; God will accomplish Micah's salvation for him – God's righteousness will bring about Micah's vindication. In light of the suffering servant's sacrifice in Isaiah 53, the New Testament writers have perceived that this deliverance has been accomplished through the death and resurrection of Jesus (see Mark 8:45; Rom 3:21–26; 2 Cor 5:21; Gal 2:16; Phil 3:9).[17] We also notice in verse 9 that even though the passage looks beyond Micah's own deliverance to the restoration of the people of God, the passage does not automatically apply this restoration to the whole nation, since repentance is required on an individual level. Only those, who like Micah, acknowledge their sin and look to the Lord will be saved.[18] Finally, the canonical text or "the Spirit of Prophecy" transcends the prophet's own experience and points to the Greater One who is to come. Like Micah, Jesus

---

17. A question may be raised here, "How can God be the accuser, the judge and the advocate all at the same time?" Of course, we should remember that the atonement as presented in the Bible is unique and does not correspond exactly with any transaction in human society.

18. Pastor Wang Mingdao, who was imprisoned for his Christian faith, reflected in his memoirs, "I was in prison for 20 years, never saw a Bible, but I am very thankful that I memorised a lot of Scriptures, the passage that comforted me the most, was Micah 7:7–9. These few verses of Scripture gave me strength and comfort."

was condemned and suffered, but God brought him into the light with the vindication of the resurrection. There is also a parallel with the preceding story of Jonah, the prophet who likewise experienced the anger of the Lord in the raging of the sea and in the belly of the fish, but who was then miraculously delivered after three days. It is interesting to note that the same Hebrew term for "rage" (*za'aph*) is used in Jonah 1:15 and Micah 7:9, where "the rage of the LORD" is in the emphatic position. In the New Testament, Jonah is also used as a type of Christ (Matt 12:39–41; 16:4; Luke 11:29–32).

Micah's experience of despair and deliverance describes the experience of every Christian who has realized the gravity of his or her own sin and that salvation depends totally on God's forgiveness and mercy. Even though sincere Christians endeavor to do justice and love mercy, all fall short and only God can provide adequate righteousness. This happens through the atoning sacrifice of Jesus on the cross.

7:11–17 The Final Day of Restoration

Whereas the previous section talked about a day of punishment (v. 4), this section talks about a day of restoration. Not only will the people of God be revived, but Gentile nations will also come to share in Israel's blessing. The expression that a day will come for "building of your walls" probably refers in the first instance to the walls of Jerusalem (see Pss 102:16; 147:2), but then also to the cities of Judah (see Ps 69:35) since it is unlikely that Samaria is being addressed here. The book of Micah has been edited after the reign of Hezekiah when Samaria had already become a ruin. People of Jerusalem, on the other hand, through the building projects of Hezekiah and Manasseh, were very familiar with the restoration and extension of walls (see 2 Chr 35:2; 33:14) (see Figure 8). This prophecy was first literally fulfilled when Nehemiah rebuilt the walls of Jerusalem in the fifth century, but the prophecy refers to more than just a physical rebuilding of the city of Jerusalem. Building is an important metaphor in the Bible that is applied to human endeavors as well as to God's intention to establish his kingdom. Humans built cities and tried to make a name for themselves (e.g. Gen 4:17; 11:4–8; Exod 1:11), but only God's house will endure (Ruth 4:11; Deut 6:10; 8:12; 1 Sam 2:35; 2 Sam 7:11–16, 27). The imagery of walls, representing a strong and well-protected city, is used as a symbol for God's people. So too, in the New Testament building imagery is frequently used as a metaphor for the church (e.g. Matt 7:24–26; 1 Cor 3:10–14; Eph 2:20–22). The main point of the passage is that after atonement has been provided for sin, God's people will be restored. In terms of biblical theology, the work of atonement on Golgotha is the cornerstone of the whole building (Ps 118:22; Isa 28:16; compare Matt 21:42; 1 Pet 2:6–8). It is interesting to note that we have the same sequence from atonement to restoration in David's prayer of confession, which concludes with the request "to build up the walls of Jerusalem" (Ps 51:18).

But it is not only cities which are going to be rebuilt, the nation's boundaries are also going to be extended. The word that is used for "boundary" (*hoq*) in the text is not the regular word for "boundary" (*gebul*), which occurs 241 times in the Hebrew Bible. Rather, the word used here (*hoq*) carries a range of meanings including portion, limit, task, obligation, rule, and statute. The usual word for boundary or border does occur in Micah 5:5, so the use of another term here calls for careful consideration. The text seems to be saying that more than a physical enlargement of Israel's territory is envisioned and suggests that Israel's influence is going to be extended beyond its traditional borders. The following line gives the reason for the extension of Israel's boundaries and corroborates our interpretation of the boundary as influence or task: great nations will come to Jerusalem (v. 12). The wording recalls the prophecy of Micah 4:1–5 where Gentile nations will come to Jerusalem to study God's law. Evidently, the text refers to the ingathering of the Gentiles into the people of God, a regular theme in the prophets. The size of the physical territory of Israel will be far too small to incorporate the populations of the great empires of Assyria and Egypt, let alone all people from sea to sea and mountain to mountain. The expression "from sea to sea and mountain to mountain" is another merismus and designates all the earth. Whereas the whole world suffers God's judgment in Micah 1:2–3, here the whole world will experience salvation. Therefore, the text does not refer to a political or physical extension of Israel's territory, rather the meaning is metaphorical. All nations will come under Jerusalem's influence and blessing (compare Isa 27:6). Also, this text, in our opinion, indicates that the time of writing was well before the Babylonian exile of Judah, otherwise we would have expected the text to refer to Babylon, Persia, or Egypt, and not Assyria. Finally, verse 13 indicates that at the same time there will be a continuation of judgment. Like the great vision in Micah 4:1–5, the biblical text does not predict that there will suddenly be a perfect kingdom of godliness and peace on earth. Rather, the Bible anticipates a historical process in which God's word will go out into the entire world until the final consummation when Jesus will return to complete his work of redemption. There will be both blessing and curse, growth and decline. The expression "as the result of their deeds" (literally, "the fruit of their deeds") refers to the natural consequences of wickedness (Mic 3:4; see also Deut 28:20; Judg 2:19; 1 Sam 25:3; Isa 1:16; Hos 4:4).

In verse 14 there is a transition to a new subsection.[19] The major exegetical question relates to the identity of the person being addressed here. Theoretically, God may be addressing the prophet, Micah could be addressing the king or other leaders in Judah, or Micah could be addressing God, in which case it would be the only prayer in the whole book. It appears that the best answer is that Micah is addressing God, since the expressions "your people" and the "flock of your inheritance" are most appropriately understood as covenantal terms with God being the sovereign master. The term "people" (*'am*) occurs 23 times in the book. It may refer to Israel (Mic 2:4, 11), to humanity (Mic 4:1, 3; 13; 5:7–8), or specifically to God's covenant people (Mic 1:9; 2:8, 9; 3:3, 5; 6:2–3). This is the only place where the expression "your people" occurs in Micah, but "my people" occurs a few times. The term "flock" occurs four times and it is clearly identified as God's flock (Mic 2:12; 4:8; 5:4; 7:14). Micah is praying that God will come down to gather, shepherd, feed, and protect his people in order to fulfill the prophecy in Micah 2:12 as well as the prophecy about the coming ruler in Micah 5:4. This hope for God to be the "shepherd" reflects dissatisfaction with contemporary kings, who were supposed to be the shepherds of Israel, and moves beyond the expectation of just a Davidic ruler but to God himself. Micah's prayer was indeed answered with the coming of Jesus, the good shepherd of God's people (John 10). Being alone in a forest underscores the vulnerability of the flock and its need for a shepherd. The geographical areas of Bashan and Gilead were renowned for good open pasture. This area formed part of the northern kingdom but had long been lost to foreign powers. If verse 14 is Micah's prayer, then in verse 15 we have God's answer. Now God is speaking and he will indeed act miraculously. The exodus tradition is recalled when God acted extraordinarily in history to bring Israel out of Egypt and into the Promised Land. God raised up a powerful prophet, performed supernatural wonders, confused his enemies, and guided Israel (Josh 3:5; Pss 72:18; 86:10; 98:1; 106:22; 119:18; 136:4). This expectation of a new exodus is very prominent in the book of Isaiah (see Isa 35:1–10; 40:1–5; 41:14–20; 43:18–21; 55:12–13).

The final two verses of the section return to the theme of the ingathering of the nations. Not only Israel will be saved in the future, the nations are also going to see God's action and are going to respond with remorse that leads

---

19. We may note the paragraph marker after verse 13 in the Hebrew Bible.

to repentance and faith. Great military infrastructures will become a shame! Especially when a nation's population is impoverished and does not have basic healthcare, education, and social welfare. The reference to the "serpent" speaks about the destruction of the evil one and his ways (see Gen 3:1, 15; Num 21:6–9; Isa 27:1; 65:25). Trembling and fear before the Lord are indications of repentance and humility (see Deut 10:12; Hos 3:5; Ps 119:161).

A SERIOUS CALL FOR CHANGE IN CHRISTIAN LEADERSHIP

Micah's sincere confession with tears challenges all pastors and preachers to examine their lives. Micah points out that the biggest problem with the world is the sin of God's people. But more specifically, he emphasizes that it is not the sin of God's people in general, but of the leaders, the priests, and the prophets. In present-day language, the biggest problem with the world, from God's perspective, does not lie with idolatrous society, but with the Christian church and especially with its leaders, pastors, and preachers. This revelation calls for serious reflection, repentance, and a return to gospel sincerity and truth. Micah exposed the sin of those who were supposed to be the examples and the guides of the covenant people; and then, after self-examination he discovered that even he himself was not without sin. We must accept, therefore, that this is also the case with us.

Indeed, when we observe the behavior and lifestyle of Christian leaders and pastors today, it is often hard to notice any difference from business or political leaders. Besides the "Christian" label, there is nothing that sets them apart from others. Repentance must start with the leaders of the church and the preachers of the gospel. We are very critical of immoral societies and non-Christian governments, we also shake our heads at the liberalism and the deterioration of the church in the West, but we do not realize that we are exactly the same. We demonstrate the same behaviors as our non-Christian compatriots such as reckless driving, copyright breaches, littering, and callousness. We emulate all the newest "Christian" fashions to be popular and draw crowds. And we are more concerned about our financial security than the spiritual health of God's people. We are very much like our neighbors, who hardly know that we are Christians. Micah calls us to return to God, to seek his kingdom and his righteousness in every area of our lives, and to embrace the life of discipleship along the road that Jesus outlined for us. How much time do we spend in prayer and the study of God's word? How much experience do we have of self-denial and cross-bearing? Can we say, like Paul, that we carry the marks of the Lord Jesus in our body? Have we become poor – like Peter, Andrew and John – for the sake of the kingdom of God?

Preachers and teachers of the gospel must rediscover God's intention for the church to be a blessing to the world, to turn idolatry into true worship, to exchange exploitation for justice, and to change cruelty into compassion. Preachers and teachers of the gospel need to realize that we fall far short from God's intentions and that judgment is already unfolding in various ways upon the church and the world. And then, most importantly, preachers and teachers must rediscover the gospel of reconciliation through what God has done in the Lord Jesus Christ. Preachers need to turn their backs on fads such as "being slain in the spirit," "the fourth dimension," ecstatic experiences, holy laughter, emotionalism, and so-called "holy fire," and get serious about real sacrificial and compassionate Christian living. They must reject the prosperity gospel and start preaching the gospel of the cross which alone is the true gospel and which alone can change the human heart and meet its deepest needs. With this kind of repentance, there is much hope for the church in Asia. Christians will rediscover the gospel, the church will revive, and righteousness, truth, and compassion will spread throughout Asia. There will be effective and true Christian witness and millions will again be drawn into God's kingdom. It will be a day for the rebuilding of walls and for the extension of boundaries.

MICAH AS A MODEL FOR TODAY

The *Book of the Twelve* is not only about the message of the Lord, it is also about the messengers of the Lord (Hag 1:13). There is, of course, a very close relationship between the message and the messenger of the Lord in the Bible (see Hag 1:13). The number twelve is not accidental, but is used in the Bible to represent the people or the servants of God, e.g. Israel had twelve tribes and Jesus had twelve disciples. The *Book of the Twelve* is representative of the message and the messengers of the Lord, providing a comprehensive picture of the prophets. Therefore, it is instructive to examine the portrayal of the minor prophets; each prophet has his own distinctive background, character, circumstances, and calling. They are all different, yet all were used by the Lord to bring his message to his people. So too, when we look at how Micah is presented, there is much instruction for preachers and teachers today. According to the three main characteristics of true prophets, we may look at Micah's calling, his life, and his message.

First of all, we notice that although Micah was from the small rural village of Moresheth, he had a very clear calling from the Lord to be a prophet. Micah is introduced to the reader on the basis of, or as the result of, "the word of the LORD" coming to the prophet (Mic 1:1). The introduction also mentions that "the word of the LORD" came to Micah "during the reigns of Jotham, Ahaz and Hezekiah." Noticeably, it was not just on one occasion, but a continuous experience in the life of the prophet. His calling could be substantiated with a series of events, indicating that God wanted him to be a prophet. Furthermore, since the text does not mention Micah's ancestry, like with some of the other prophets (e.g. Isaiah, Jeremiah, Ezekiel, Hosea, Joel, and Jonah), we assume that his family may have been without distinction in Israel. Nevertheless, Micah had a deep conviction that the Lord called him to the task of preaching and continually experienced the enabling power of the Spirit in his ministry (Mic 3:8; 7:8–10). Therefore, according to the book of Micah, Micah's qualification for being a prophet resides in divine calling and divine enablement, not in family pedigree or social status. We also notice that Micah, living in Moresheth, was very much integrated with society; he lived among the common people and faced the same hardships of daily life (Mic 7:1–7). He was not a stranger or lived a separate life from the people of God. It is interesting to observe that the calling of the disciples in the New Testament corresponds to Micah's experience. The disciples were not people of distinction in terms of family lineage or social position, they lived ordinary lives among the common people, and they experienced the Lord's call on numerous occasions in their journey.

Secondly, whereas Micah's life had much in common with ordinary people, it was quite different from the other leaders, priests, and prophets. Most of the clergy lived the "high life" at the expense of justice and mercy. They were corrupt and exploited their ministry positions for their own material and social

Micah 6–7: The Message of Reconciliation

advantage. Micah, however, was very different from the average prophet and lived a life of integrity and righteousness (Mic 3:8). He had spiritual depth and an unsullied moral life. Yet, we note that Micah was humble, and the first one to confess his own shortcomings and sins (Mic 1:8–9; 7:8–9). He did not parade himself as being above the common people or as being holier than them. In addition, Micah, like Moses, was also a suffering servant. Living among the common people in rural Judea, he knew what it meant to be exploited and oppressed. He experienced antagonism, and perhaps even persecution, from false prophets who demanded that he stop proclaiming judgment (Mic 2:6). In a society of corruption and unfaithfulness, a prophet lives a lonely life. He goes against the cultural trends and does not cheer the newest fashions. But, more importantly, Micah also felt the pain of Israel's sin and God's judgment. He was a prophet who suffered, lamented, and repented on behalf of the people (Mic 1:8–9; 7:9). Although Israel sinned and Micah warned them, when judgment came Micah did not revel in his fulfilled prophecy, but experienced it with pain. He lived in the reality of the judgment he pronounced. His experience expressed his deep concern and love for the people of God and reflected God's heart. In this respect, he was unlike Jonah who yearned for the condemnation of Nineveh. And, finally, we may observe that despite suffering and the bleakness of his current situation, Micah retained faith, remaining confident in prayer and hope (Mic 7:7). The key to his perseverance was of course his relationship with the Lord (Mic 7:18–20). Again, when we look to the disciples in the New Testament, we note that their lives too were characterized with integrity, purity, and sacrifice.

And, thirdly, Micah's message focused on God's agenda with respect to salvation history and the coming of the Messiah, rather than on petty personal or even national concerns (Mic 4:1–4; 5:2–5). He faithfully exercised his ministry of proclaiming God's message. He was a keen student of God's law, immersed himself in the prophecies of the time, and spent much time in God's word in order to proclaim God's message truthfully. Whereas the false prophets talked about themselves and social prosperity, he spoke about the coming Messiah and God's future kingdom of peace. He did not have all his treasures on earth, while exhorting others to have their treasures in heaven. His preaching was consistent with the way he lived, hence he was taken seriously. Micah did not compromise his message nor his lifestyle, but despite opposition courageously spoke on God's behalf. Indeed, it was the Spirit who strengthened him for this task (Mic 3:8). Jesus' disciples in the New Testament, as demonstrated in their writings, also focused on the proclamation of the gospel and did not pursue selfish or worldly agendas (2 Cor 4:5).

But, ultimately, Micah's calling, lifestyle, and ministry point to the Lord Jesus Christ, who is the perfect embodiment of mercy, justice, and God himself. Truly, the question inherent in Micah's name, "Who is like the Lord?", finds its complete answer here. In Jesus, the messenger and the message of the Lord merge perfectly together.

7:18–20 Doxology: Final Vision of God

Verses 18 to 20 conclude the chapter and provide a doxology to the whole book of Micah. Indeed, it is very fitting that the book concludes with a description or vision of God. The question, "who is a God like you?" echoes the meaning of Micah's name and the main theme of the prophecy. Of course, the implied answer is "No one!" No one or nothing can be compared to the Lord. The question also recalls the Song of Moses (Exod 15:11; see also Deut 3:24; 2 Sam 22:32; Ps 77:13), which celebrates the power of the Lord in destroying the Egyptians. Remarkably, when we look at the following verses, which summarize the *leitmotif* of the whole prophecy, we note that it is not God's power or holiness that is highlighted, but his grace. He forgives sin! The clauses "who pardons sin" (literally, "forgiving iniquity") and "forgives iniquity" (literally, "passing over rebellion") are expressed with two participles, indicating continuing action. God's characteristic activity is to forgive sin, much more so than condemning sinners straightaway when they do evil. Certainly, for there to be any hope, this is precisely the kind of God that humanity, who has a propensity to sin, needs; especially God's rebellious people. The word "transgression" or "rebellion" is the same word used in Micah 1:5 which describes the basic problem of God's people (see also Micah 3:8). The message of Micah is that God is going to resolve the problem; on the one hand, he is going to judge rebellion, but on the other hand, more amazingly, he is also going to forgive and pass over the sins of his people. This is consistent with the portrayal of God in the rest of the Old Testament (see Exod 34:7; Num 14:18; Ps 103:8; Isa 33:34; Jer 9:23–24; Joel 2:13).

Additional consideration of the two participles will enrich our understanding even further. The first participle, usually translated as "pardoning" (*nasa*), literally means "to lift," "to take away" or "to carry." All these meanings are illustrated in the book of Micah (Mic 2:2, 4; 4:1, 3; 6:16; 7:9). From these basic nuances the word has also come to be used for the bearing of guilt (e.g. Gen 4:13; Lev 5:1, 17) as well as that of forgiveness, i.e. the removal of guilt (e.g. Gen 50:17; Exod 32:32; Ps 32:5). Therefore, from a New Testament perspective the clause, literally meaning both "pardoning iniquity" and "bearing iniquity," is a picture of Jesus on the cross bearing the sin of the world in order that forgiveness may be procured (see John 19:17; Heb 9:28; 1 Pet 2:24; 1 John 2:2). This picture also reminds us of the book of Leviticus which teaches that there cannot be atonement without sacrifice, for example the scapegoat was made to bear the iniquity of Israel on the Day of Atonement (Lev 16:22). In the same way, the verb "passing over" does not mean that God simply ignores sin, rather it recalls the Passover ritual where a lamb was slaughtered and its blood sprinkled on the doorposts so that the angel of death would pass over the house (Exod 12:1–50). Since it is on the basis of the shed blood of the Passover sacrifice that Israel was delivered, it is evident that the idea of atonement lies behind the meaning of "passing over." Again, in the New Testament Jesus becomes the Passover lamb who through his sacrificial death provides for the cleansing and forgiveness of sins (Rom 3:35; 5:9; Eph 1:7; Col 1:20; Heb 9:14, 22; 13:12, 20; 1 John 1:7; 1 Pet 1:19; Rev 1:5; 5:9).[20] Therefore, at the end of the book of Micah we are brought to the foot of the cross. Indeed, we may ask "who is a God like you?" We can only humbly bow with gratefulness, admiration, and worship.

The final sentence of verse 18, "You do not stay angry forever, but delight to show mercy," also invites comment. The verb usually translated as "he delights in" (*haphets*) occurs only once in Micah, but is very common in the rest of the Old Testament occurring 123 times. Although its basic meaning is generally given as "to take pleasure in," it is significant to point out that this meaning extends into the idea of "to plan." In some contexts, this nuance is to the fore (e.g. Judg 13:23; Ruth 3:13; 2 Sam 24:3; Job 13:3; Pss 115:3; 135:6; Eccl 8:3; Isa 44:24; 53:10). Similarly, the noun *haphets* which is derived from the verb is translated as "delight," but also often more appropriately according to the context as "plan" or "counsel." Therefore, the expression "he delights in mercy" also incorporates the idea that "he plans for mercy." In fact, the verb is in the perfect tense (i.e. the Hebrew past tense) and so we may translate it as "he planned to exercise mercy." Consequently, the answer to the question, "why does his anger cease?" is "because he has planned to be gracious." The point is that the Lord does more than simply delight in mercy; he has also already planned to act according to his mercy and grace.

Verse 19 repeats the main point of verse 18 with memorable poetic imagery. God is more inclined towards mercy than judgment, and therefore will again turn to show compassion to his people as he has done on numerous occasions throughout history. As God relented from bringing judgment upon Nineveh, so too he will be merciful to his people (Jonah 3:9; see also Deut 13:18; 30:9). The word "compassion" occurs only once in Micah, but it reiterates one of the main themes of the Book of the Twelve which was introduced by Hosea (Hos 1:6–7; 2:3; see also Isa 54:8). Indeed, it is for this reason that sinners may persevere in serving God, otherwise they might as well give up

---

20. These ideas are also clearly expressed in Isaiah 53.

(Psalm 130:4). So too, Calvin comments, "God forgives the remnant of his heritage, because he is by nature inclined to show mercy."[21] But God will not only forgive their iniquity, he will also subdue it just like the Israelites subdued the Canaanites in the land and kept them under control, so too sin will be overcome and restrained in the lives of God's people. The expression that God will "hurl all our iniquities into the depths of the sea" also recalls the Song of Moses and Israel's deliverance from the pursuit of the Egyptians (Exod 15:1, 4–5, 8, 10, 19). It indicates that there will not only be full remission of sin, but also complete victory over sin. The problem of sin in Israel, that brought failure and judgment, will disappear forever (Mic 1:5; see also Mic 3:8).

With the final words of the prophecy in verse 20 the prophet reminds the reader of God's faithfulness and mercy. The terms "faithfulness" and "mercy" regularly occur in poetry in parallel construction as a word-pair (Pss 25:10; 26:3; 36:5; 40:10–11; 57:3; 61:7; 69:13; 85:10; 86:15; 88:11; 89:1–2, 14, 24, 33, 49; 92:2; 98:3; 100:5; 108:4; 115:1; 138:2; 143:1; Prov 3:3; 14:22; 16:6; 20:28). God's faithfulness pertains to the certainty that he will fulfill his covenantal promises, and since he will do what he has promised, mercy will be the result. In the same way, the faithfulness that Jacob experienced, even though he was a cheat, stems from God's covenant mercies to Abraham. Despite Israel's rebellion, God's mercy and grace will overcome all their failures (Ps 117:2). According to Paul in Romans 15:7–12, this promise of faithfulness and covenantal mercy has been fulfilled in Jesus. Again, the prophet recalls the "days long ago." As God has promised and acted in the past so he will act in the future. Micah leaves the reader with the vision of God's faithfulness and grace. It is now up to the reader to decide how to live in the present.

The book of Micah encourages us to recapture our vision of God: to know who he is, what he has done in history, what he intends to do in the future, and especially what he is doing now. Despite our indifference and worldliness, God still forgives and restores. In his love, he remains faithful and will fulfill all his promises. God is almighty, majestic, and infinite; yet, God's greatest distinction is his mercy, his willingness to forgive, and his enduring love. Micah has shown us at the beginning of his prophecy that the great problem of the world is the sin and idolatry of God's people (Mic 1:5), and now at the conclusion of his prophecy he shows us that the solution lies in God's faithfulness and mercy. Of course, the doxology points us to the gospel of the Lord Jesus Christ. In him all God's promises are fulfilled and in him we may find the forgiveness

---

21. John Calvin, *Commentary on Jonah, Micah, Nahum*, 245.

Micah 6–7: The Message of Reconciliation

of sins and receive a new heart to live for God. A rediscovery of the gospel is the only hope for the church and for the world.

Micah's final vision of God also teaches us that the greatest things in life are not outward success, power, or splendor, but mercy, forgiveness, and love. Many Asian cultures, adopting the idols of the West, have become fixated on affluence and military power, often seeking after dominance and revenge. It is not surprising that many Asians do not talk about forgiveness, because true forgiveness can only be found in the gospel. Only those who know God and follow Jesus possess this powerful virtue. Similarly, it is unfortunate that many churches are pursuing worldly agendas of size and affluence, exchanging real spiritual riches for filthy rags. Micah, however, presents a different kingdom and an alternative set of values. There is a new realm of righteousness and peace, based on God's grace and faithfulness, and governed by the ruler from Bethlehem. This divine kingdom is already here, steadily spreading throughout Asia, and millions are beginning to experience its power. God is forgiving and reviving his people, and they are becoming like dew and rain nourishing parched ground. This kingdom is spreading to the ends of the earth, and more and more people are entering a new future. Micah leaves the reader with the vision of God's grace and rule, it is now up to the reader to decide how to respond.

SELECTED BIBLIOGRAPHY

Alfaro, Juan I. *Justice and Loyalty: A Commentary on the Book of Micah*. Grand Rapids, MI: Eerdmans, 1989.

Allen, Leslie C. *The Books of Joel, Obadiah, Jonah, and Micah*. NICOT. Grand Rapids, MI: Eerdmans, 1976.

Andersen, Francis I. and David Noel Freedman. *Micah: A New Translation with Introduction and Commentary*. AB. New York: Doubleday, 2000.

Calvin, John. *Commentary on Jonah, Micah, Nahum*. Grand Rapids, MI: Christian Classics Ethereal Library, 1999.

Childs, Brevard. *Biblical Theology of the Old and New Testaments: Theological Reflection on the Christian Bible*. Minneapolis: Fortress, 1992.

Childs, Brevard S. *Introduction to the Old Testament as Scripture*. Philadelphia: Fortress, 1979.

Harris, Laird R., Archer L. Gleason, and Bruce K. Waltke. *Theological Wordbook of the Old Testament*. 2 volumes. Chicago: Moody Press, 1980.

Hasel, Gerhard F. *The Remnant: The History and Theology of the Remnant Idea from Genesis to Isaiah*. 2nd ed. Andrews University Monographs, Studies in Religion, Volume 5. Berrien Springs, MI: Andrews University Press, 1974.

Hillers, Delbert R. *Micah: A Commentary on the Book of the Prophet Micah*. Philadelphia: Fortress, 1988.

House, Paul R. *The Unity of the Twelve*. Sheffield: Sheffield Academic Press, 1990.

Kaiser, Walter C. *Back to the Future: Hints for Interpreting Biblical Prophecy*. Eugene: Wipf & Stock, 2003.

Kaufmann, Y. *The Religion of Israel*. Abridged and translated by Moshe Greenberg. Chicago: University of Chicago Press, 1960.

Keil, C. F., and F. Delitzsch. *Commentary on the Old Testament, Volume 10: Minor Prophets*. Translated by James Martin. Grand Rapids, MI: Eerdmans, 1973.

Kugel, James L. *The Idea of Biblical Poetry: Parallelism and Its History*. New Haven: Yale University Press, 1981.

Limburg, James. *Hosea-Micah. Interpretation: A Bible Commentary for Teaching and Preaching*. Atlanta: John Knox Press, 1988.

Lowth, Robert. *Lectures on the Sacred Poetry of the Hebrews*. London: S. Chadwick & Co., 1847.

Luther, Martin. *Luther's Works, Vol. 17. Lectures on Isaiah 40–66*. Edited by Hilton C. Oswald. Philadelphia: Fortress, 1972.

Mangalwadi, Vishal. *The Book That Made Your World: How the Bible Created the Soul of Western Civilization*. Nashville, TN: Thomas Nelson, 2011.

Moberly, R. W. L. *The Old Testament of the Old Testament: Patriarchal Narratives and Mosaic Yahwism*. Minneapolis: Fortress, 1992.

Petersen, David L., and Harold Richards Kent. *Interpreting Hebrew Poetry.* Minneapolis: Fortress, 1992.

Prior, David. *The Message of Joel, Micah and Habakkuk.* The Bible Speaks Today. Edited by J. A. Motyer and John Stott. Downers Grove: InterVarsity Press, 1999.

Pritchard, James B. *The Ancient Near East. Volume 1 & 2: An Anthology of Texts and Pictures.* Princeton, NJ: Princeton University Press, 1973.

Sanders, J. A. *Canon and Community: A Guide to Canonical Criticism.* Philadelphia: Fortress, 1984.

Schmidt, Alvin J. *How Christianity Changed the World.* Grand Rapids, MI: Zondervan, 2001.

Shaw, Charles S. *The Speeches of Micah: A Rhetorical-Historical Analysis. JSOTSup Series* 145. Sheffield: Sheffield Academic Press, 1993.

Smith, Ralph L. *Micah-Malachi.* WBC, Vol. 32. Dallas, TX: Word Books, 1984.

Vawter, B. *Amos, Hosea, Micah, with an Introduction to Classical Prophecy.* Wilmington, DE: Michael Glazier, 1981.

Villanueva, Federico. *Psalms 1-72: A Pastoral and Contextual Commentary.* Asia Bible Commentary Series. Carlisle, UK: Langham, 2016.

Waltke, Bruce K. *Micah: An Introduction and Commentary.* TOTC. Leicester: IVP, 1988.

Whiston, William. *The Works of Josephus, Complete and Unabridged.* Peabody, MA: Hendrickson, 1987.

Wolff, Hans Walter. *Micah the Prophet.* Translated by Ralph D. Gehrke. Philadelphia: Fortress, 1981.

Asia Theological Association
54 Scout Madriñan St. Quezon City 1103, Philippines
Email: ataasia@gmail.com Telefax: (632) 410 0312

OUR MISSION
The Asia Theological Association (ATA) is a body of theological institutions, committed to evangelical faith and scholarship, networking together to serve the Church in equipping the people of God for the mission of the Lord Jesus Christ.

OUR COMMITMENT
The ATA is committed to serving its members in the development of evangelical, biblical theology by strengthening interaction, enhancing scholarship, promoting academic excellence, fostering spiritual and ministerial formation and mobilizing resources to fulfill God's global mission within diverse Asian cultures.

OUR TASK
Affirming our mission and commitment, ATA seeks to:

- **Strengthen** interaction through inter-institutional fellowship and programs, regional and continental activities, faculty and student exchange programs.
- **Enhance** scholarship through consultations, workshops, seminars, publications, and research fellowships.
- **Promote** academic excellence through accreditation standards, faculty and curriculum development.
- **Foster** spiritual and ministerial formation by providing mentor models, encouraging the development of ministerial skills and a Christian ethos.
- **Mobilize** resources through library development, information technology and infra-structural development.

To learn more about ATA, visit www.ataasia.com   or   Facebook /AsiaTheologicalAssociation

Langham Literature and its imprints are a ministry of Langham Partnership.

Langham Partnership is a global fellowship working in pursuit of the vision God entrusted to its founder John Stott –

> *to facilitate the growth of the church in maturity and Christ-likeness through raising the standards of biblical preaching and teaching.*

Our vision is to see churches in the majority world equipped for mission and growing to maturity in Christ through the ministry of pastors and leaders who believe, teach and live by the Word of God.

Our mission is to strengthen the ministry of the Word of God through:
- nurturing national movements for biblical preaching
- fostering the creation and distribution of evangelical literature
- enhancing evangelical theological education

especially in countries where churches are under-resourced.

Our ministry

Langham Preaching partners with national leaders to nurture indigenous biblical preaching movements for pastors and lay preachers all around the world. With the support of a team of trainers from many countries, a multi-level programme of seminars provides practical training, and is followed by a programme for training local facilitators. Local preachers' groups and national and regional networks ensure continuity and ongoing development, seeking to build vigorous movements committed to Bible exposition.

Langham Literature provides majority world preachers, scholars and seminary libraries with evangelical books and electronic resources through publishing and distribution, grants and discounts. The programme also fosters the creation of indigenous evangelical books in many languages, through writer's grants, strengthening local evangelical publishing houses, and investment in major regional literature projects, such as one volume Bible commentaries like *The Africa Bible Commentary* and *The South Asia Bible Commentary*.

Langham Scholars provides financial support for evangelical doctoral students from the majority world so that, when they return home, they may train pastors and other Christian leaders with sound, biblical and theological teaching. This programme equips those who equip others. Langham Scholars also works in partnership with majority world seminaries in strengthening evangelical theological education. A growing number of Langham Scholars study in high quality doctoral programmes in the majority world itself. As well as teaching the next generation of pastors, graduated Langham Scholars exercise significant influence through their writing and leadership.

To learn more about Langham Partnership and the work we do visit **langham.org**

Lightning Source UK Ltd.
Milton Keynes UK
UKHW02f1837240718
326220UK00004B/8/P